Truth, Spirituality
and Contemporary Issues

Lesley Parry

Hodder & Stoughton
A MEMBER OF THE HODDER HEADLINE GROUP

Acknowledgements

I'd like to thank the following for their help in this book. Firstly, to JRH for support, criticism and everything generally. To Swifty for her ideas and support. To Janet D for her proof-reading skills. I hope the book helps in the pursuit of GCSEs, and also opens interest into what is happening all the time, but we never notice.

The publishers would like to thank the following individuals, institutions and companies for permission to reproduce copyright images in this book: Angulimala: p83; AP: p12 (left) and (right); BBFC: p69 (2nd from top,left), p73; Bridgeman Art Library: p8 Lauros Giraudon; Corbis: p71 (3rd from top) and (7th from top) and (bottom), p86 (bottom), p87 (left), p89 (top, left) and (bottom, middle), p6 (bottom) Nigel J. Dennis, p6 (top) Bill Varie, p7 (bottom, right) A & J Verkaik, p8 (top, right) Michael S. Yamashita, p8 (bottom, left) Paul Edmondson, p12 (bottom) Chris Lisle, p19 (left) Elio Ciol, p20 (left) Michael Freeman, p20 (middle) Paul A Sauders, p20 (right) Dave Bartruff, p21 (left) Shaldan Collins, p21 (right) Rose Hartman, p23 (right) Danny Lehman, p30 (top) Andrew Brookes, p30 (bottom left), Novimages/Corbis Sygma p55 (bottom) Jeffrey L. Robman, p56 (top) Massimo Mastrorillo, p61 (top) Leland Bobb, (middle) Larry Williams and Associates, (bottom) John Henley Photography, p71 (top, left) Jose Luis Peleaz, p79 Liba Taylor, p86 (top) Chase Swift, p89 (bottom, right) Rick Gomez, p19 (bottom) and p94 (left) David Turnley, p94 (right) Joseph Sohm, Chromosohm Inc., p95 Annie Griffiths Belt; Corel: p7 (top, left);Church Action on Poverty: p96;Crisis: p91; HarperCollins Publishers Ltd(1950)/C.S. Lewis: p21 (bottom); Hello Limited: p68 (bottom, left); Liverpool Football Club: p18; National Blood Service: p38; © News International Newspapers Limited (September 6): p68 (top, left) and p68 (top, middle); PA Photos: p18 (left), p56 (bottom), p78 (bottom) EPA, p80 (top) and (bottom), p81, p89 (top,right) and (middle, top); Photodisc: p68 (bottom, right), p69 (top, right) and (top, left); Photofusion: p62 (top) Ian Simpson, p62 (bottom) and p78 (top) Paul Baldesare, p63 (top)

Ray Roberts, (bottom) Julia Martin; Popperfoto/Reuters: p97 (right) Kimberly White; The Ronald Grant Archive: p30 (right), p69 (2nd from top, left), p70 (top) courtsey Warner Bros/Paramount Pictures, p71 (4th from top) courtesy Matt Groening/Fox TV, and (6th from top), p75 C4; The Salvation Army: p24, p97 (top) and (bottom) Gary Freeman;The Samaritans: p44; Science Photo Library: p32 (top) Don Fawcett, and (bottom) BSIP, Veronique Estiot, p33 (top) Phillipe Plailly/Erelios and (bottom) Jerry Mason, p55 (top) J.C. Tessier/Publiphoto Diffusion, p57 Sue Baker, p59 Martyn F. Chillmaid, p60 (middle) Dr. P Marazzi, and (bottom) Erika Craddock; S. Leutenegger, © Ateliers et Presses de Taizé, 71250 Taizé-Communauté, France: p23 (left); Streissguth, A.P., Landesman-Dwyer, S., Martin, J.C., & Smith D.W. (1989). Teratogenic effects of alcohol in humans and laboratory animals. Science, 209 (18): 353-361: p60 (top);Topham Picturepoint: p69 (2nd from bottom, left) and (2nd from bottom, right), p70 (left), p71 (2nd from top) and (5th from top), p89 (bottom, left); World Jewish Relief: p98; BBC Worldwide: p68 (bottom, right).

The publishers would also like to thank the following for permission to reproduce material in this book: Church Action on Poverty for extracts from *www.church-povrty.org.uk*; ASH; The Prison Reform Trust for extracts from *www.prisonreformtrust.org.uk*.

Every effort has been made to trace and acknowledge ownership of copyright. The publishers will be glad to make suitable arrangements with any copyright holders whom it has not been possible to contact.

Orders: please contact Bookpoint Ltd, 130 Milton Park, Abingdon, Oxon OX14 4SB. Telephone: (44) 01235 827720. Fax: (44) 01235 400454. Lines are open from 9.00 – 6.00, Monday to Saturday, with a 24 hour message answering service.

British Library Cataloguing in Publication Data

A catalogue record for this title is available from the British Library

ISBN 0 340 850345

First Published 2002

Impression number   10 9 8 7 6 5 4 3 2 1

Year   2008 2007 2006 2005 2004 2003

Cover photo from Photodisc.

Typeset by Liz Rowe.

Printed in Dubai for Hodder & Stoughton Educational, a division of Hodder Headline Plc, 338 Euston Road, London NW1 3BH.

Contents

➤ Introduction
Truth, Spirituality and Contemporary Issues

This book is written to meet the specification set by AQA as **Specification B Module 4**. This is a totally new course, and has no guidelines beyond the specification outline and sample paper. It is likely that the Principal Examiner will shape the paper into a recognisable form, which allows predictions to be made as to its content and style after a few years. However, we are not at the point where we can do this, and so must follow the Specification. This textbook aims to do just that.

Written as a companion volume to **Thinking about God and Morality**, I have produced a textbook of similar style in that it will meet the specification, but will also encourage students to think about the points they make and issues they meet. It provides information from both secular and religious viewpoints, but encourages the students to assess and evaluate those responses, as well as to develop their own.

The book follows the specification set in terms of its order of content, but each Unit is separate to allow any order of Units as suits a Centre. As with **Module 1 Thinking about God and Morality**, not all topics are to be answered in the final exam. This gives an element of choice to those studying this Module, and therefore those using the book. The Units are written with this in mind, in that they give complete information for each individual Unit. Common to thinking behind the Modules, better candidates are expected to see and comment on links between topics within Units themselves and between Units. The book makes at least some of those links explicit to increase the depth of understanding held by such students, as well as introducing greater depth to others, who I hope will be able to make use of it. It is essential that the book provides a depth of information for teachers, since much of this Module is new to GCSE. This reflects a desire by AQA to provide a cross-curricular course.

The content of the course is designed to enable Religious Studies to link closely with other subjects, particularly Citizenship and Personal, Social and Health Education, and to contribute actively to pupils' Spiritual, Moral, Social and Cultural development (AQA Specification p39).

The book will be split into two halves, comprising nine Units, as follows:-

Section 1 Nature and Expression of Truth and Spirituality
Unit One   Nature of Truth and Spirituality
Unit Two   Claims to Truth
Unit Three Expressing Spirituality in Society

Section 2 Religious Responses to Contemporary Issues
Unit Four   Religious Attitudes to Matters of Life
Unit Five   Religious Attitudes to Matters of Death
Unit Six   Religious Attitudes to Drug Abuse
Unit Seven Religious Attitudes to Media and Technology
Unit Eight Religious Attitudes to Crime and Punishment
Unit Nine   Religious Attitudes to Rich and Poor in Society

Various religious traditions will be met within the book. As with Module 1, religious traditions acceptable to the course are specified. These are the major world faiths (Buddhism, Christianity, Hinduism, Islam, Judaism, Sikhism) and the major denominations of Christianity (Anglican, Orthodox, Protestant, Roman Catholic). Candidates must study either one or two traditions for each Unit, and in the 'Contemporary Issues' Units, a Christian tradition plus one other (Christian or world faith). The book allows Centres to choose, from a range, the traditions they prefer to use in addressing the topics. This recognises the fact that some Centres choose to study only Christian traditions, whilst others prefer a multi-faith approach. It must be pointed out, though, that the exam rubric demands a Christian response within every answer, so two Christian responses will be provided for each topic.

The issues of exam rubric and technique within response will be considered in the book, since these are vital things to get right. Students with good exam technique do better than those without, as they know how to best answer a question, what questions are really asking, etc. As for exam rubric, many candidates lose marks every year because they have answered the wrong number of questions, or used unacceptable combinations of religious traditions, or have failed to understand exactly what the question is asking. Comments and guidance within the book, and sample questions and answers will address this need.

A revision guide/matrix is found at the end of the book. This helps candidates to see exactly what to revise. Additionally, the sample paper produced by AQA is included to enable candidates to become familiar with its style. There is also a glossary of words. It is important for candidates to be able to use and recognise technical terms. It would be helpful for any candidate to learn these words as part of their study and revision.

1 The Nature of Truth and Spirituality

What is Truth?

I am 16 and was born in Billinge.

My mum and dad are always rowing. I expect they'll divorce eventually.

I have a sister and brother.

I am gay. There should be an equal age of consent — 18 for everybody.

I'll be a vet if I complete my studies to the right standard.

I play rugby for a local youth team. Man of the match in the last six games puts me top of our 'Best Player' table.

Euthanasia is murder — you can't just end a life.

I believe all our rules come from one ultimate source in the end.

I like Chinese food best.

I believe in reincarnation, after reading some Buddhist stuff.

This is Zak, and he's telling you some true things about himself. Do a diagram of yourself like the one above. There must be lots of things you can say about yourself.

Look at Zak's comments. Are they all true? How do we define *truth*? What sorts of *truth* does Zak use here? What sorts of *truth* have you used about yourself? Do you think they'll still be truths in five years? What does that tell you about *truth*?

Types of Truth

There are many ways to see something as true. For this course, you need to know about four types of *truth*. Make sure you learn them!

It'd be wrong to just pocket this, I should hand it in.

Use the chart to help you determine what type of truth is being used by each of the following people:-

Fred – Jesus' parable of the Good Shepherd shows God is love.

Sue – The number of people in England in 1066 is known because of the Domesday Book.

Steve – Liverpool FC won three major Cup competitions in 2000-2001.

Carly – Through astronomical observation, we know that the earth moves around the sun.

David – In most societies, any form of drug abuse is considered wrong.

Helen – We know that there are four distinct seasons in terms of British weather.

Chris – God created the world.

Amy – Murderers should be executed.

The Basics

① What are the four types of *truth*?

② Explain each, and give an example to show your understanding.

③ What problems can there be with each truth?

④ *Science is the only truth.* Do you agree? Explain your answer.

Evaluating Truth

Look back at the types of truth on the previous page, and at the statements. Each speaker is stating what is, for him or her, the truth.

Do you believe all the statements to be true? Why do you think you might differ?

Different truths are important for different reasons. With a partner, try to think of times when each type of truth might carry most importance.

The importance with which I hold a type of truth will affect my attitude and behaviour. For example, as a member of certain faiths, I will not agree with post mortems. I will believe that this is interference, and damages what God has created. Even though the law in my country might say that a post mortem must be carried out, I will not give my consent to that for a member of my family. My spiritual truth based on my religion is the most important.

Read the newspaper report. What sorts of truths are being stated? Which one(s) should have had priority? Which one(s) do you think were effective?

From the newspaper report, you can see several important ideas. Firstly, that the most important types of truth don't always carry the

MAN CLEARED OF RAPE WALKS FREE

Today in court, Bob Jones walked free, relieved that his ordeal was over. He had been found not guilty of the rape of a 23 year-old student. During the trial, the Police had demonstrated that Jones had had sex with the student, through DNA tests. The student of Theology had sworn on the Bible that she had been raped, and that Jones had ignored her pleas to stop. Jones' defence was able to make a strong case that the student was consenting, through the way she behaved and the clothes she wore. It was later revealed that Jones had been convicted of a sexual assault some five years previously. However, the court system had not allowed the jury to know this in the trial. ■

most weight where they should. In a Court of Law, a person should be convicted based on the evidence given (historical truth), and a scientifically based theory to show the course of events. At times, though, those truths can be overshadowed by appealing to people's sense of morality.

Thus, at times less relevant truths can be most effective. Hence we can see that different truths at times clash. Look at the scene below. What sorts of truths might be being considered in it? Which ones will carry most impact?

Each of the truths is important, and significant. They all help people in different ways. They also create problems. What ways do they help? How do they create problems?

Evidence ... Proof ... Probability ... Certainty ... Belief ... Trust ...

For the exam, you need to be able to compare the various strengths of the truths considered. It isn't as straightforward as it would seem – scientific proof doesn't always win the day – after all it is only a description of observed regularity given set conditions. If the conditions change, the truth is no longer the same, e.g. gravity doesn't exist in space, so things don't drop! Some people have superstitions. The truth of their superstition comes from within themselves. No matter how much scientific or historical evidence you provide, they don't lose that superstition.

The way we view a truth will determine how much hold it has over us. If I am religious, I'll believe in God. The fact that scientifically I can't prove God exists doesn't matter. I know God exists as a spiritual truth, and I know much historical evidence for Him (*such as?*). Anyway, two-thirds of the world's population can't be wrong! This is where we use evidence to prove things to ourselves and others. This allows us to say what is probably true or what is a certainty. Learn the heading words and their definitions.

Look at the pictures. Match the picture to the correct word.

Read the text below. It will help you to understand the use of the terms. Can you make up sentences about yourself using each word appropriately? Pick out the problems with each statement.

*My work over the two years was the **evidence** I could do Physics, and that I'd get a good result. My mum **trusted** me to sort out my revision programme and to get on with it. My teacher had told her if I did the work I was **certain** of a good grade, and that she **probably** didn't need to worry about letting me get on with it myself. I was bright and mature in my attitude, I could be relied upon. They **believed** in me.*

*I failed – the **proof** they were wrong. I had too many other things to think about when I should have been revising...and I didn't need that result anyway, so I thought.*

Definitions

Evidence – grounds for belief/disbelief; the data on which to base proof or to establish truth or falsehood

Proof – any evidence that helps to establish the truth/validity/quality etc.

Probability – likelihood; although you can't be certain, you can hypothesise that something is likely

Certainty – inevitability

Belief – principle/idea accepted as true or real, especially without positive proof

Trust – reliance on and confidence in the truth/worth/reliability of a person or thing

Make a list of things that are certain, and things that are probable. Would you gamble on a probability? What about on a certainty? Is there a difference?

Religious Faith

There is no empirical evidence (scientific truth) for God's existence, yet over 70% of the world believes in religion. Religions come from God, so the view which shapes a believer's decisions, practices and life is said to come from God. Why do religious people stick to these views then, when they go back to an idea, not a fact? Well, they are convinced of God's existence because of many things. Events in their lives may have given extra support to their belief. This makes compelling proof of God's existence, certainty has been reached. Check this conversation out:

Definitions

Reason – the faculty of rational argument/deduction/judgement

Experience – direct personal participation/observation; actual knowledge/contact

Faith – strong or unshakeable belief in something/someone

Sara – Phil, why do you believe in God?

Phil – My folks brought me up that way. They believe in all that stuff.

Sara – So did mine, but I changed my mind. My gran died.

Phil – My brother died – bone cancer. I know God looked after him then and carries on doing so now. He comforted me at that difficult time.

Sara – You can't prove God exists.

Phil – My Bible tells me about Him, how He created the world, how He wants us to live. It is infallible. You can't prove He doesn't.

Sara – The Bible is a story book.

Phil – And anyway, I went to a meeting the other week. The guy speaking was visited by God, and told to bear witness.

Sara – That's a good claim to fame!

Phil – The morning after the meeting, the sunrise woke me up – so early is unusual for me. I feel God was telling me to get on with my new life with Him. God's creation is wonderful, don't you think?

Sara – I think nature is beautiful, but not all the time.

Both make assumptions: they start out with a premise, and demonstrate others through the course of their conversation. Phil concludes that God exists, Sara that He doesn't.

Can you spot the assumptions and premises? Will they ever be able to agree? How might they each view the following events?

1 plane crash, 4 survivors, 164 dead
2 a friend claiming to have been visited by God whilst studying
3 people struggling in a famine hit country.

Faith versus reason

Which is stronger – faith or reason?

Everyday, we use reason to work things out. Can you think of some examples?

Everyday, we rely on our faith even more! Today you might have got up believing there was sufficient hot water to wash … believed your parents had made provisions for your breakfast … dressed appropriately for the weather you believed we'd have … believed your journey to school would be smooth … it is endless. Life is about a multitude of acts of faith – and that is without being religious! What acts of faith have you shown today?

Let's go back to the original idea – God's existence is a spiritual truth, which can have immense impact on my way of life. The other part of this Unit looks precisely at that.

The Basics

① Define evidence, proof, certainty, probability, faith, belief, reason, trust.

② For each word, give a sentence to show your understanding of it.

③ What is the difference between evidence and proof? Probability and certainty?

④ *Faith is not reasonable.* Do you agree? Explain your answer.

What's the Meaning of Life?

Science tells us we exist because of a mechanical process. Some of us are planned by our parents, but really they are just letting nature take its course. In an average lifetime, we are born, live for 70-80 years and die. The first 30 years see our continual growth, then ten years of equilibrium, before we enter a phase of decline, which ends with our personal extinction. Nothing survives in any personal sense other than other people's memories of us (and they disappear eventually too) or something we may have made/done. There is no reason, purpose, or value to our existence. We – you – are one of millions of just another species on the earth. You may be individual, but that is not because you were made that way – it is a combination of chances, DNA, upbringing, country of birth, experiences… You are nothing more than a being distinguishable from animals by the ability to rationalise. Birth, life, death – the end.

Spot the difference

How does the idea above make you feel? Does it explain life adequately to you? Do you want there to be more?

Most people want there to be more. They want there to be…

- a purpose to our existence
- a reason for our existence
- something more than just our bodies
- a further life after this one
- some ultimate justice which rights the wrongs seen on earth
- some greater power who looks after them

These are ultimate questions. Religions attempt to answer them. Maybe that is why religions began.

Do you think religions were invented to provide answers to those ultimate questions? What does that tell you about God?

More Than This?

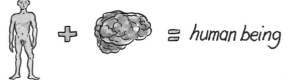

Is there more to life than the physical reality which science tries to map for us? What evidence could you give to suggest there is another dimension or side to the story?

If you think about it, in terms of humans, it makes a difference, especially if you believe in life after death. If I'm going to come back to life, or have a new life, there has to be something separate to my body – it rots, gets old, gets hurt. Zombies aren't many people's idea of a fun life after death! In other words, we wouldn't want to have our bodies back – we need something a bit less limiting and limited.

Most religions talk of the soul or spirit. This is the permanent part of us, the part that makes us what we are (personality, self, etc). It is our spiritual side, but we can't prove scientifically that it exists. You can't do an autopsy to find a spirit, though most people believe they have one.

Why do some people want there to be more than just their bodies?

Find out about the idea of the soul/spirit in one religious tradition. Put your notes with your work.

Awe ... Wonder ... Mystery

Look at the pictures on this page. How do they make you feel? What do you associate with them?

The words heading this page are often used in the context of nature. They are words to describe the feelings evoked by nature. Many people believe that God reveals Himself through nature. Nature is God's creation, and just as artists reveal their ideas and style through their work, so God reveals elements of Himself through nature. When we look at nature, we can be amazed by the complexity within it – the tiniest area can have hundreds of different species of life within it, all co-existing. We can be stunned by its beauty – think of flowers, landscapes, baby animals. We can be overwhelmed, even frightened by its power – a storm, for example. We can feel peace and stillness within it – imagine sitting in a forest in the early morning. Science can explain how things work, and every day can explain a little more, but much remains a mystery. The biggest mystery of all is perhaps how it all turned out the way it did, when an explosion was supposed to have been its origins.

Such things as these often make people feel close to God.

They can feel touched by God or in touch with God. Nature is a revelation of God.

Those who have studied Module One of this GCSE specification may already recognise the above. Rudolph Otto is perhaps the most important scholar to consider this idea. He knew that he could not prove God existed, yet he was convinced that God does exist, and that he had met/experienced God many times. He claimed that in the world we could gain a sense of God in many ways, and he called this the *numinous*. Those feelings of awe, wonder and mystery all come from experiencing God in the world and nature. They are the *numinous* at work.

Have you ever seen something you wanted to photograph it was so beautiful/amazing?

How do you think the idea of the numinous may have contributed to the origins of religion? Did the sense of awe and wonder lead people to ask those ultimate questions, and then to create religions to answer them? Does it all flow from God, so that we have come to the idea of God through experiences of God?

The Inner World...Creativity and Inspiration

Have you ever had to do creative writing in an English class? Or had to draw a picture using your imagination in Art? What about play a sport and do something out of the ordinary to turn a game round for you or your team?

Welcome to the inner world of creativity and imagination, inspiration and insight. It is the world where children and artists feel at home, but most of us – as we mature – try to keep locked away. It is the source of our spirituality. But where does that creativity have its origin?

Religions will tell us that we can contact some element of God within us, which is the root of our spirituality. This triggers a response to the things around us, and finds expression in the creative elements of our nature. Many artists and musicians, for example, claim to be inspired by God. One American pastor, Craig Pitman, has tried to increase acceptance of artists within Christianity, claiming they have God-given talents, and their work is an expression of God. The work of many of these people is clearly religious. Frank Wesley is a New Zealand artist who expresses his religious belief through his paintings. Dennis Stephen is a Christian musician who writes his own material in a contemporary style to try to communicate what he sees as God's message to the world.

For both, the inspiration they feel through God's presence in their lives leads them to express their spirituality through their work.

Are people guided by God to produce this work (a direct revelatory stimulus)? Or does the world inspire them to search within themselves, which leads to the expression of that search through art? Where does your stimulus come from for creative work/thinking? Is there something special within each of us that this relates to or comes from? What is that?

Orthodox Christianity is a religious tradition which really shows off its spiritual side. Go into an Orthodox church – it is beautiful. The walls are so ornate and decorated and magnificent paintings adorn the building. These paintings – icons – are very special. Their production involved meditation and prayer – the artists should have been focused on the idea of God during their making.

In Buddhism, tangkhas are painted. Although Buddhism does not profess a belief in God, these paintings draw on the spiritual search of their painter. They rely on his/her meditation and focus on Buddhist truths and teachings.

Both of these are about contact with that inner self – a spiritual search.

Everything Counts

Most religious traditions share the idea of treating others the way you would like to be treated. This is known as the Golden Rule. Do you agree with it?

The rule, of course, has a prerequisite – you have to love yourself first, that is, feel that you yourself are worthy of being treated well. This allows you to want others to be treated well too. It comes from a belief in your own personal self-worth. When Jesus told people that the second most important rule was to *Love your neighbour,* he added the rider *as you love yourself.* Even ancient religions told their followers *Know thyself* (inscription over the oracle at Delphi).

Why do you have to love yourself to be able to love others?

All religions tell us how valuable we are as individuals. The need to feel valued and loved is one of the reasons why believing in God is a comfort to many. Look forward to Units Four and Five to see comments from different faiths about the sanctity of life.

Why are we special? Think of what religious people might say, as well as non-religious.

The belief that we are special can come from the belief that God created each of us uniquely and individually. Your DNA, fingerprints, iris, and personality all testify to that as a fact. An accompanying belief is that the world was created for us to use and to take care of. Therefore, all of nature is also special. Altogether there is nothing that is not of value – everything counts.

The Buddha spoke of seeing a ploughing contest as a child. Instead of feeling the excitement of the competition, he felt sadness at the suffering of all within it – including the worms being cut by the ploughs. All the beings within the contest – direct or indirect participants – had enough worth to provoke this feeling within him.

If we feel that all has value/worth, how might that affect the way we live our lives — our behaviour and attitudes? What does this tell you about people who cause destruction?

The Basics

① Write out some of the questions considered to be ultimate questions.

② Why do some people feel that humans are more than just a physical body?

③ Explain the idea of the numinous, with examples to aid explanation.

④ How might the following answer the question of where we get our creative ability? Religious person; artist; atheist.

⑤ Use quotes to demonstrate that people have individual value/worth. How does this have a knock-on effect in viewing the world?

Touching Base ... Meeting God?

Meditation is about reaching the very still part which exists within each of us. Some would call it being grounded or centred. Many would say that it is really a sense of contact with the Divine within.

In early Christianity, the Gnostics believed that we each held a piece of God within us, and our spiritual search should be leading us to be reconciled with God. Hindus believe that God is within each of us.

It seems that any spiritual journey leads us deep within ourselves. It can be a very emotional journey, which creates all kinds of feelings. As Francis Huxley said, 'there we must deal with awe, fascination and terror, with ignorance shot through with the lightning of certainty, and with feelings of exuberance, love and bliss ...' All feelings you might expect if you met God.

Why?

Where exactly the journey leads depends on our own interpretation. Think of the artists – where does their inspiration come from? Does the painter of an icon come close to the Divine in the creation of a new work of art? Does it stop at our soul (if we have one!), or is there more? Does our creativity, which animals patently do not have (when did your cat last write a best selling novel?!), prove that we have a soul?

A Simple Meditation

Try this for 10–15 minutes.

Sit in a quiet place where you can't be disturbed. Sit with your back straight, legs uncrossed (unless you are sitting on the floor). Put your hands together in your lap. Now close your eyes. Breathe normally. Try to count the number of breaths you take, each time counting the out breath. Just follow your breathing, don't try to make it even or to regulate it in any way. If you lose count, just start again – don't worry. You will have thoughts coming into your head – what was that noise? What must I look like? Let the thoughts come, and let them go, don't chase them. You are trying to be still, and to reach that calm centre within.

After doing this how do you feel? Peaceful, calm, relaxed? Those who meditate regularly do so for far longer than 5 minutes, but it is always beneficial.

God Within?

I realised early in the service that something was not right. I looked around, everyone was singing normally, yet I felt choked. I had to get out before I exploded. I walked to the vestry, shutting the service out, and sat down. I began to weep for the burden I was suddenly aware of carrying – all my past transgressions. Then I felt a light, and a voice. I can't say I saw or heard them – I felt them and they were real. The dialogue let me be freed of my burden, and I felt light and whole. I felt so loved and so strong. I would have invited Christ into my life there and then, but I realised I didn't need to. He had been there all along, I just hadn't noticed. It was as if I was uncovering a precious jewel within myself, which had long lain in wait, still and knowing. As I left the vestry, I felt quiet, centred, at the end of one journey, and on the brink of the next.

Exam Tips

In the second half of this section, you might have noticed a distinct lack of written tasks, yet a lot of thinking required. Spirituality is an inward journey about personal reflection, not academic papers. As Dot Thomson, a General Advisor for an LEA says, 'Talking about Spirituality is like shifting a mountain of sand with chopsticks – very difficult. We haven't adequate language to express what makes up spirituality – beliefs, feelings, emotions, thoughts'. This makes life particularly difficult for those of you doing an exam which includes the topic of spirituality! You need to be aware of the general ideas within the topic (the page headings will help in that respect), and be able to think around the ideas. Flexibility of mind is most helpful here.

If you have already studied a Module from this GCSE course, you will be familiar with the style in which you should answer questions. Simple knowledge questions require simple responses. It is usually one mark per correct response, with no explanation required – unless specifically stated. The next type of question is through Levels of Response. These require developed answers, which give breadth and depth of response to gain above half the available marks. A specific form within this type of question is the evaluative question. These require you to answer from more than one point of view.

Try some of each. You can use the table in Appendix 1 on page 101 to help you see how to answer this sort of question.

Knowledge Questions

1　What are the four types of truth?

2　Give an example of each.

3　Define these words – certainty; belief; evidence; reason.

Thinking Around a Topic Questions

4　Why are some truths stronger than others?

5　Why do some people feel the need to believe in a God?

6　How do religions guide their followers in the truth?

7　Why do some people believe we are more than our bodies?

Evaluative Questions

8　*All inspiration is God-given.* Do you agree? Give reasons to explain your answer.

9　*Meeting God must be a blissful yet terrifying experience.* Do you agree? Give reasons and show you have considered more than one point of view.

10　*Humans are just another species – nothing more, nothing less.* Do you agree? Give reasons and explain your answer.

2 Claims to Truth

For the course, you need to understand the sources of authority followed by religious believers. These are varied, and have varying degrees of control for religious believers. There are three areas within the course – religious authorities; sacred writings; and conscience.

Religious Authorities

This is sub-divided into three –

The *institution*, which is the organisation founded for the specific purpose of expressing the beliefs and teachings of that faith/denomination.

The *traditions*, which are ideas held by that faith/denomination. They might be in written or oral form, and often shape practices, e.g. how to do something.

The *leaders*, who hold positions of responsibility within that faith/denomination. They are often believed to have been given their position by God.

Let's explore four religious traditions to find those elements.

Sikhism

There are five major temples in the Punjab, which provide authority and guidance for Sikhs on major issues. The leaders of the five major temples, who will consult holy books, and relevant experts, make up the Council of Five. The Council has existed since early times within the faith, and their pronouncements have become part of Sikh tradition. However, it has no absolute authority – only the Guru Granth Sahib holds that. On a day to day basis, Sikhs might go to speak to a granthi for advice. A granthi knows and can read the Guru Granth Sahib, but has had no formal training in the teachings of Sikhism. They might refer to the Rahit Maryada, which is the Code of Discipline for Sikhs. This tells Sikhs how to live and behave – it is tradition in written form. It is considered to be responsible for uniform Sikh practice across what is a worldwide community, which demonstrates its effectiveness.

Roman Catholic Church (Institution)

The RC Church believes in apostolic succession, that is, in the early church the disciples passed on the truth about Jesus and the authority to preach God's message to chosen ones following them. This authority was passed on via ordination. This means that the RC Church – its leaders and hierarchy – can claim to be in a direct line from Jesus' disciples. The Pope, or Vicar of Christ on Earth, is the overall leader of the RC Church, and according to Vatican II acts as spokesman for all of the other bishops. Vatican I had declared in 1870 that on certain matters and when speaking ex cathedra, the Pope speaks for God, infallibly. One of his roles is to maintain the traditions of the RC church. Those traditions link back through history, so are very important. Many were said to have been given by Jesus himself, so are unchanged. The official voice of tradition is known as the magisterium of the church.

Islam

There are many schools of thought within Islam, but no institution in the same way that the Roman Catholic church has. The absolute authority is the holy book – the Qur'an – and no one can replace that. Leaders of the community are called Imams, and they can guide and support Muslims. All Muslims follow the Shariah, Islamic Law. An institution within Islam constantly reviews and updates it to ensure it covers all aspects of life. They make use of tradition, which is found in the Hadith and Sunnah to help interpret the Qur'an appropriately. The people within this group are all well-respected leaders within their own right. Islam is a way of life as well as a faith, and so any leaders are both religious and political. The Ayatollah of Iran is a good example of this, and his pronouncements carry great authority.

Judaism

In Judaism, the rabbi (religious leader) is an important figure. He/she has studied the Jewish scriptures in depth to be able to explain the law to the members of his/her synagogue. Their advice and guidance is greatly respected. The degree of acceptance varies though – Orthodox Jews see it as binding, whilst Reform Jews see it as advice. Tradition plays a major part in Judaism. There are many books about the Minhagim of Judaism – the customs, and where they came from. These traditions give extra protection to the laws, keep Jews mindful of the law, and allow Jews to show even greater devotion to God. For these reasons, they are very important. They are also an historical link to Jews throughout history – something very important to the Jewish faith. Jews can look to the institution of the Bet Din for further guidance, e.g. on matters of Kashrut, but a major decision on the faith would require a Sanhedrin – a gathering of major Jewish leaders from the whole world. This is not a likely event.

The Basics

① For the following, explain how and why they are important, and give examples from two religious traditions to demonstrate the points you make :-
a. religious institutions
b. religious traditions
c. religious leaders

② For the following, explain why reliance on their authority might cause problems. State what the problems might be and give examples from two religious traditions to demonstrate the points you make :-
a. religious institutions
b. religious traditions
c. religious leaders

These ideas might help you – different leaders might say different things; the power of the institution; power the institution claims leader has; different interpretations; one overshadowing another; forgetting the original holy book text. Think about how important or authoritative things/people can become or can be allowed to be.

Sacred Writings

Sacred writings are holy books. These writings are considered holy or sacred because of their link with God. At the least, they are descriptions of God, His work and what He wants of His people; at the most, they are the result of God's dictation, via angels or Himself. Let's look at some interpretational differences.

The Holy Bible

This is the sacred writing of Christianity. Many believe that the Holy Spirit oversaw its writing and compilation. It is made up of two halves, and a number of individual books. The first half is the Old Testament – a book of law, prophecy and history. It tells the story of the Israelites, and their relationship with God, and leads to the second half – the New Testament. This is the story of Jesus and his message. It also describes the earliest spread of the new Christian religion.

The Torah

The sacred text of Judaism, found in scroll form in every synagogue in the world, this is the name for the five books of Moses. The Torah is considered to be the infallible word of G_d. Torah signifies guidance and instruction, and includes the 613 mitzvot, or laws of Judaism. It is considered to include everything a Jew would need for life – ethics, justice, religion and education – and as such, study of it by every Jew is expected. Following the laws was part of the Jewish covenant with G_d. The Torah is seen as G_d's communication with man – G_d reaching out to man. By following the laws, man reaches out to G_d. Its relevance is absolute and eternal.

The Qur'an

The holy book of Islam. This was recited by Muhammad ﷺ, who had been taught the recitation by the angel Jibrail. Qur'an means recitation. Although translations exist in many languages, these are classed as translations, and not as the holy book. The original language of the Qur'an is Arabic, and Muslims should try to learn it in that language. It is considered to be the infallible word of God, and is seen to speak to all people in all times. Its guidance covers all aspects of life, and its rules should be followed without question, since they are direct from God.

The Guru Granth Sahib

This is the holy book of Sikhism. It comprises hymns and poems by the Sikh Gurus plus material from non-Sikh sources. It is a book in praise of God, and gives advice about how to live as God wishes. The Guru Granth Sahib is written in Gurmukhi script, a language created for it, based on the spoken language of the region. The book is available only in its original language and in a set format to preserve its status. Sikhs believe it to be divinely inspired scripture, not just human writing. It has absolute authority.

How Can We Interpret Sacred Writings?

The first, and most basic interpretation is to see them as the result of direct revelations from God. Since God is infallible, and these are His utterances, they too are infallible. This means they are completely correct in every way, and they are appropriate for all people, in all places, at any time in history. They should not be changed in any way, because to do that is to know better than God – humans can't know better than God. What does this mean for the rules within the book?

One such understanding is seen in the doctrine of *sola scriptura*. This states that holy scripture is the only source of all knowledge of what God is/wants. God hasn't left us, His creation, to work it all out ourselves, but has provided guidance for us. It provides everything we need to know in this world to follow God and to attain heaven, because it is a true record of what God has to say to mankind, which never changes.

Secondly, we can interpret them as being divinely inspired, though not dictated. The writers have written a truth, which people can understand, which has come from God. The stories may not be written in a scientific way, rather as poetry or in story form, but they still contain God's message, which is the truth. There may be errors because man has made mistakes in their writing, but they still provide us with the truth.

Thirdly, we can interpret them as being God's words, which must be interpreted by man. God guided the writers, perhaps through general as well as specific revelations. Much should be taken as spiritual rather than literal truth. People made sense of the message they received and put it into a form that others could understand – parables, hymns, poems etc. It is not to be taken as the literal word of God.

What does each mean for the rules of the holy book?

The Basics

① In what different ways does God create holy books?

② Name two holy books, and write about their contents and interpretation.

③ Do you think religious believers would follow their holy book more closely if they held a particular view of how it was written? Explain yourself.

④ What difficulties may be caused for a believer by holding a particular interpretation? Explain yourself.

Conscience

What is that? Any ideas?

The Oxford reference dictionary states, 'conscience is the sense of right and wrong that governs your thoughts and actions'. It is difficult to describe exactly. There is no organ within our body that a doctor could point to on a scan and say, 'there you go – that's your conscience'. In fact, there is no physical proof of it!

Can something exist if there is no physical proof?

We all accept we have a conscience. It's that little voice in our heads which advises us, isn't it? Where does it come from? Does the fact that we can't actually physically locate it mean that it is external? In that case, where (who) is it from?

Some people believe that we acquire an idea of right and wrong – a morality – through our upbringing, combined with our experiences throughout life. All the times we are told something is right or wrong, or we see or feel that something is right/wrong/good/bad adds to our own personal morality. As a class, choose an issue, and see if everybody perfectly agrees on every single detail. It's doubtful. So our sense of morality is individual, though we share a general morality. That sense of morality forms our conscience – it is a product of our social environment and socialisation. Further evidence to support this is that as we get older our ideas change, which coincides with more varied experiences. For example, I might strongly disagree with euthanasia, until someone close dies after a painful and undignified struggle through cancer. Then, even if I still don't believe in taking life, I might feel that sometimes killing someone is the right option. (See forward to Unit Five, p41–54.)

Many religious people believe that our conscience is actually a way in which God can communicate directly with us, if we allow Him to. God can guide us via our conscience. Many people make claims for religious experiences; some, such as Mother Teresa, claim to be guided throughout their lives by God. It would seem logical that if our conscience came from an external force, it would be from God. Our conscience may be part of our sub-conscious identity. A non-physical God would interact with that.

Do you agree? Can you argue for and against that idea?

Some things to think about...

► If God is my conscience, what about when it tells me to do something that is considered wrong?

► Descartes proved God's existence by showing that people all over the world share a common morality, even without having had any contact. Is this evidence of God communicating via our conscience?

► Does a person's morality change? So, does that mean your conscience does too?

Exam Tips

This Unit will be met in the first question on the exam paper. It is a compulsory, stimulus response question. Stimulus response means you are given one or more statements, images, or quotes to think about. These are to do with the actual questions asked. They are often referred to in questions, and should act as triggers to help you. The whole of the question will usually be split up into three types of questions – straightforward definition type questions (what is…?); questions asking you to apply your knowledge (why do some people say…?); and evaluative questions (do you agree?). At the end of Unit One, you saw these three types – all the questions on the paper will have them. Here we are going to specifically look at the evaluative questions.

These are marked via their own Levels of Response criteria. There are other Levels of Response questions on the paper, but they have a different set of criteria, which we'll meet later. There are five levels within the type we are considering here, and answers are worth 5 marks maximum. Their wording stands out, and they try to lead you to the full mark available.

• They start with a quote, which you are asked to agree or disagree with. If this is all you do, you'll get no marks. The examiner's interest is your reasoning only.
• So, the question will ask you to explain your answer, giving reasons to show why you agreed/disagreed.

• It will ask you to give more than one point of view. If you only agree or disagree, you must think, and write, about why others might have the opposite view.
• Later Units may use the phrase *Refer to religious teachings* in evaluative questions. You must do this, or you won't be able to get full marks.

In Appendix 1 of this book (p101), you'll find a grid, which might help you to see more clearly how these questions are marked. Use it to construct answers when you are revising.

Try some…

1 *Religious believers should always follow the guidance of their leader, because they have been chosen by God.* Do you agree? Give reasons and explain your answer, showing you have thought about more than one point of view.

2 *Holy scriptures provide guidance, not instruction, so needn't be followed to the letter.* Do you agree? Give reasons and explain your answer, showing you have thought about more than one point of view.

3 *I believe my conscience is God.* Do you agree? Give reasons and explain your answer, showing you have thought about more than one point of view.

3 Expressing Spirituality in Society

Introduction

This Unit builds on the previous two Units. Religious people believe in religious and spiritual truths. These truths may or may not be able to stand up to scientific testing, but that does not matter to their believers. When you think about it, it is illogical to believe that science could prove their truth, when science doesn't have the tools to demonstrate God, which is where the spirituality comes from.

This Unit asks you to be aware of some of the ways in which people express that spirituality, and those religious beliefs. It also wants you to be able to describe some of these ways from two different religious traditions.

Some of the elements within this Unit will link to other Units. For example, you have to know about support of Voluntary Organisations – in the Issues Units, you also have to know about these organisations. The top candidates are able to use ideas from other Units to support what they say, as well as from the Unit specified by the question. Bear that in mind, when you meet those ideas again.

So What are Some of the Ways People Express Their Spirituality?

It can be a difficult question to look at with no prompting. However, you are likely to be able to drag out some examples from your memories of RE in earlier years – given the right motivation or help.

Let's look at it from a different angle. My spirituality is really what I am; it is often a reflection of my deepest or strongest beliefs and feelings. In that sense, everyone has a spirituality, which they express in their daily life.

Some people might say that football is the new religion. So how do football fans express this 'religion'? They dress in their team's colours, becoming an instantly recognisable group, which even appears to have a dress code. They hold season tickets, and travel to as many games as possible home and away, providing support for each other and the team. They have rituals to perform on match day, which they believe to mystically aid their team. They write stories or music for/about their team, or draw pictures of the players. They hold their club's credit card, and are Supporters' Club members. All of this shows their allegiance and devotion, and is an expression of this 'spirituality'.

For the examination, you have to know about how religious people express their spirituality – talking about a football fan is unlikely to get you many marks! So how do religious people express their spirituality? Read on …

Expressing Spirituality by ... Symbols

What is a Symbol?

It is something which represents something else. For the course, you'll need to know some examples and what they represent.

Religious Artefacts

An artefact is an object or tool, which has been crafted by someone. These have religious significance.

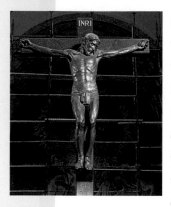

What religious objects can you think of? Split a page into six for each of the major faiths. Can you think of items for each religion? With a partner, can you add to your list? Can the class come up with any more? Do you know how any of them are used?

Roman Catholics carry crucifixes, which are crosses with the figure of Jesus on them. They remind the holder of Jesus' sacrifice of his own life for the sake of all people. This is the foundation of their faith.

Muslims carry prayer beads, or tasbi, to focus the mind before prayer . There are ninety-nine beads altogether, which represent each of Allah's names.

Ritual Objects

These are items used in acts of worship, which have a function, as well as symbolic value.

Do the same exercise for ritual objects as you did for artefacts. Don't worry that some items appear in both lists – some artefacts are ritual objects too, or vice versa.

Christians generally use the Bible within worship – in procession (showing its importance), to read from it (receiving God's guidance), or sometimes just to kiss it (to gain a blessing).

Jewish men wear tefillin during prayer. Tefillin

are small leather boxes strapped to one arm and their forehead. They contain a small portion of scripture, which is the Jewish declaration of faith. Their positioning reminds them to love G_d with head and heart.

Physical Movements

Here the examiner is referring to the fact that there are set patterns of movement used, usually during acts of worship, by many faiths.

Can you think of any? Try to do the same task again but for 'physical movements' this time. It is the hardest one, so don't panic if you can't think of (m)any!

Muslims pray in exactly the same way every time they pray. They follow a set of ritual movements, which were given by Prophet Muhammad ﷺ himself, called a 'rak'at'. The movements include bowing, kneeling, prostration and reciting the Qur'an. The Muslim shows complete devotion and submission to Allah.

Roman Catholics genuflect when they enter/leave a church. This means they face towards the altar, and whilst bending their right knee slightly, bow. It shows their respect for God.

three

... **Piety**

Piety means *dutiful devotion to God and observance of religious principles*.

In this context, we are talking about people expressing their spirituality by being pious, by carrying out acts of devotion. Quite often, it refers to particular religious practices, which people do regularly, even daily.

You need to know about three specific, but linked, areas – meditation, discipline, and mysticism.

Religious *meditation* is the act of focusing, or reflecting deeply, on spiritual matters.

Meditation is a central practice of the Buddhist faith. Most Buddhists meditate on a daily basis, so that it is a form of discipline really. It concentrates the mind, so that spiritual truths can be appreciated. For Buddhists, it is one part of the path to Enlightenment, which is their goal.

Some Christians meditate. For example, some Catholics focus on their rosary beads to draw them deeper into prayer.

Discipline is a person's regular practice of something. Religious people show discipline, because they always keep to the practice – it is a part of their (daily) existence. They often carry out activities in such a way.

Muslims pray in a way that shows total discipline of the body and mind. They complete five prayer sessions every day of their lives (unless ill), at set times each day, following a set physical pattern every time, and in set numbers of those patterns for each prayer session.

Many Roman Catholics attend Mass every day. It is important to renew their promises to God, and to carry out an act of self-cleansing every day. The daily rituals demonstrate their devotion to their beliefs.

Mysticism is a system of thoughtful prayer and spirituality which aims at gaining direct contact with God. It is a pattern of belief and behaviour designed to gain special revelations of God.

St Teresa of Avila (1515–82) is one of the most famous Christian mystics. Whilst a nun, she experienced God, and chose to dedicate herself to Him. It is clear that she used meditational prayer, which progressed her rapidly in a spiritual sense. She wrote several books about her spiritual journey. She claimed there were levels within the soul which you had to reach by meditational prayer, and appreciate to be able to fully realise God.

Sufism is Islamic mysticism; one group within which is the whirling dervishes. These are men who have trained in a disciplined way, so that they can spin around for lengths of time. Whilst spinning, they meditate, going into trances. In these trance states, they hope to realise spiritual truths. Some Muslim rulers were known to seek guidance from Allah through the trances of the dervishes.

... Creativity

You have already met this idea in Unit One (pages 1–11). There you read that many religious people have been inspired by God or by their surroundings and feelings to show their spirituality through the expressive arts. The examination requires you to be aware of these creative ways in which people feel drawn to express themselves. Let's add to the examples you already have, through the four categories we are offered by the syllabus – art, literature, music, and architecture.

Buddhist monks spend many years learning to create patterns and images with coloured sand. These mandalas express Buddhist spirituality. The monk will meditate in preparation for making them, and whilst making them. They are made as an act of devotion. However, they don't last – sand blows away, and is easily disturbed. The use of sand is deliberate – it reminds everyone of the impermanence of everything.

One of the most famous Christian writers of modern times was C S Lewis (1898–1963). He lost his Christian belief as a schoolboy, but regained it in his late twenties. He wrote prolifically, producing fiction work for adults and children, as well as defences of Christian belief, and other theological works. Perhaps to young people, he is best known for his seven 'Narnia' books. These contain clear Christian ideas and themes, but not in a way which seem to force the religion on the reader.

A Sikh act of worship is a very musical affair. Perhaps one of the most important roles is that of the ragi, who is a singer/musician. In the service, ragis sing and play devotional music, to help the congregation understand its message. Their faith and spirituality inspire their ability to do this, and the music they produce.

Some of the greatest buildings in the world are religious buildings. They can be breathtaking in their beauty, provoking awe and wonder within anyone gazing upon them. Most architects of these buildings have built them with a sense of God in mind. Their spirituality has found expression in their work. The Blue Mosque in Istanbul is such an example, with its many domes, minarets, and fabulous calligraphic and geometrically designed artwork. The magnificence of the building is a tribute to Allah's magnificence, the domes stressing again and again that Islam is for all people, and the calligraphy putting the words of the Qur'an into beautiful art forms.

The Lion, the Witch and the Wardrobe
C. S. LEWIS

The Chronicles *of* Narnia
FULL-COLOUR COLLECTOR'S EDITION

Collect some examples of how people have expressed their spirituality through these areas, to give extra examples for your own use in the exam. Here are some starters — Kahlil Gibran; Gaudi's cathedral; John Bunyan; rangoli patterns; Tibetan Buddhist butter sculptures.

... Membership of Faith Communities

What do we Mean by Community?

What types of communities do you belong to? How do they differ?

You could say that every person is involved to varying degrees in several different communities – home, village/town, school etc. Each has its own code of behaviour, maybe its own dress code, perhaps its own morality. We move from one to another, changing chameleon-like to fit in. Community is the label for the group we are part of at any one time.

Religious people belong to religious communities, which may be additional to those just mentioned. A symbol of that belonging is usually some sort of initiation ceremony, for example, confirmation in Christianity or the Amrit ceremony in Sikhism. The ceremony marks the switch from one life-state to another, for which considerable preparation has been made. It is a commitment to the faith, and living as part of the faith community is the expression of spirituality and faith.

There are different types of religious community, each of which requires a bigger commitment than the last. Commitment includes supporting the community and its members, worshipping as a group, living by given rules, some element of witnessing to the faith, and usually an element of service to others, which is a core value to all religions.

For the exam, you have to know about the types of community, and how people express their commitment to those communities. This, of course, is also a spiritual commitment, because it comes out of a belief in the faith and its codes, as well as a desire to live out that faith.

Denominational Communities

Most Christians are part of a denominational community, that is, a community that all attend a specific church, and come to know each other well. Any group, which attends the same place of worship and lives by its codes, can be similarly classed. Basically, the qualification is this attendance, though many will have been enrolled or initiated as adult members. Members of a Parish Church hold many events to raise money for the upkeep of the church. They provide social and pastoral support for each other, and help the older members of their community. All are Christians, and live their lives individually through their interpretation of their faith.

Faith Communes

Some groups create specific areas, where all within the area are part of the faith. They agree to live by the rules of the area. Examples include Taize in France, and Corrymeela in Northern Ireland. Neither commune is really a lifelong home, but believers go there to be immersed in the atmosphere and culture. The commitment is bigger than in denominational communities because members have to live by the rules, and are expected to contribute to the sustenance of the community itself (not just the focal place of worship).

Taizé in France *(www.taize.fr)* is an ecumenical monastic community that has grown to become a place where all are welcomed. Visitors share for a few days in a simple life with discussion around Bible texts and an act of worship three times each day. Its aim is to bring all people together, all Christians, all people.

The desire of its founder is for it to be a 'parable of communion' – a place where people seek to be one with God every day. The community accepts no donations, and there is no employed staff, so all the practical work involved in welcoming large numbers of young people is done by the community and by the visitors themselves.

Corrymeela *(www.corrymeela.org.uk)* is much more of a virtual community, in that it gives support in many parts of Northern Ireland. However, it has a base community, where people can follow residential courses. Its aim is to unite the two sides, and create a peace for Northern Ireland, and it has won many awards in recognition of its work.

Monastic communities

This type of community requires the greatest commitment, because it dictates the whole way a person lives and behaves, including mapping out most of every day for each member. Strict codes exist, which must be followed. In some ways, it may be an easier community to live in – everyone models the rules, so they are easier to keep.

Monastic communities are single sex. By having both sexes together many will be distracted from their spiritual path. All members will have gone through a period of several years of preparation before they finally decide to ask to be accepted. Acceptance leads to a ceremony where strict vows are taken – celibacy and poverty being common – and rules are acknowledged as being completely binding. Communities are often self-reliant, cut off from normal society. Members live a life of contemplation, as well as maintaining the fabric of the community itself. Buddhism has a long tradition of monastic communities, stretching back to the Buddha himself. Christianity also has a strong monastic tradition, with many Orders, such as the Benedictine Order *(www.stanbrookabbey.org.uk)*.

Think about it

- Which is more difficult – living as a Christian in a denominational community or in a monastic one? Give reasons and explain both sides of the argument.

- How is communal life a mix of the other two types?

- Which could you live in? Why?

... Support of Voluntary Organisations

Religious people are often seen to provide much help for others. Many Christians give money (or other forms of help) on a regular basis, including as a covenant. Many of the major organisations involved in such help are also linked to a religious tradition.

Can you think of the names of any voluntary organisations? Split them into obviously religious and non-religious ones.

Orphanages and hospices both came out of religious motivation, as did schools. So why do religious people and groups feel a need to be involved in such work?

> 2. Jesus helped those in need. He didn't give money, rather he directly helped them. I am a medical volunteer in Africa. I view my patients as Jesus did his, but also remember that Jesus said whatever we do to them, we do to him. By helping, I express my belief in that as a truth.

> 1. It's my duty as a Jew to help others. In Leviticus, we are given many laws as to how we must help the poor, for example. By following the law, I show my love of God.

Can you think of any more reasons?

So, how do people help?

Can you make a list of ways that people could/do help? Are any of those ways unlikely to be used by religious groups? If yes, why?

> 3. I donate to Amnesty International, who fight for justice and equality. These concepts are key to Islamic teaching, and are qualities of Allah. I show my devotion to Allah, and my belief in the importance of these concepts, through my contributions.

Your list may be huge, but all within it can probably be put into one of several categories – donations (money, material goods, own time); political work (campaigning, petitions, demonstrations); educational (informing others); prayer.

Which types of support do you feel are most appropriate for religious people? Why? Are there any which show more personal devotion than others? How?

Giving is an expression of people's spirituality. Businesses give to charity, gaining good publicity, but they also gain tax relief! Ordinary people – and we include religious people in that – feel moved to give. Something within them is saying *this is a good cause, and deserves my support*, so they give – money, goods, time etc. It is often said that we are judged by our actions – giving sends a message that we are compassionate, want fairness and equality, and want to be of help to others – all spiritual motivations.

Your regular gift will help families in crisis all year round

To make your regular gift, please fill in the banker's order form below and return it to:
The Salvation Army, FREEPOST, Bristol, BS38 7SS in the envelope provided.

Please pay The Salvation Army the sum of:
£10 ☐ £15 ☐ £25 ☐ or £ ___ (my preferred amount)
monthly ☐ quarterly ☐ twice yearly ☐ annually ☐
starting on: day ___ month ___ year **2001** until further notice.

Payable to: HSBC, PO Box 648, 27-32 Poultry, Princes Street, London EC2P 2BX (40-05-30T)
to the credit of the Salvation Army Trustee Company No 2 a/c 61638343.

Account number ☐☐☐☐☐☐☐☐   Sort code ☐☐ ☐☐ ☐☐

To: (name and address of your bank) ___ Postcode ___

Signature ___ Date ___

FOR BANK USE ONLY: Please quote ref: ___

Please return this form to The Salvation Army in the envelope provided, NOT to your

three

Exam Tips

How do we go about preparing for this topic? Firstly, know specific basics – what all the words mean and examples of each. Next, how is each an expression of spirituality – this is the examiner asking you to apply your knowledge. Finally, think about the comparative value of each – are any greater expressions of spirituality than others (more obvious, more committed, requiring more effort, gaining more grace)?

Do you know what all the words mean? Test yourself – symbolism, piety, creativity, support, membership. If you don't understand the words, you can't answer questions they figure in.

Go back through the Unit, and complete the following revision table. You can add any extras you know, but try to have at least two for each.

Expression via	Type of	Example	Religious Tradition
Symbolism	Artefacts	Rosary Beads	Roman Catholic

Apply your knowledge, ask yourself how each of the examples on your table is actually expressing spirituality. Use these questions as a guide –

- How do religious objects express a spiritual truth?

- What does a believer's support of a charity tell us about them?

- In what ways does living as a monk express one's spiritual nature?

What about comparing them? This is an evaluative style question, and so you need to have several opinions or views to offer the examiner. Try some –

- Do some forms of expression show more clearly a person's spirituality than others?

- Can these expressions of spirituality be fairly compared?

- 'More commitment means greater spirituality'. Do you agree?

When you are revising, build up your knowledge and understanding of a topic by going through those three areas – the basic meanings, the application of these ideas to real life, and the weighing up of an idea or statement. Candidates who can only do the first will get the lower grades; candidates who can do all three get the highest. You choose.

Introducing the Contemporary Issues

So, you are now into the second chunk of the course. The first part of your examination paper will test you about Truth and Spirituality – the three earlier Units of this book. The second section of the paper is made up of a series of structured essay questions on six topics. You choose to answer three of these. Those Units are the subject of the next chunk of this book, and since they make up the biggest part of the course, they'll make up the biggest part of this book.

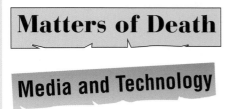

Matters of Death

Rich and Poor in Society

Media and Technology

Drug Abuse

CRIME AND PUNISHMENT

Matters of Life

Those are the six Units to study. This book attempts to introduce each to you, and to give religious attitudes to each. You will be helped by being aware of any organisations which focus particularly on any of them. That kind of knowledge helps to extend your answers, and so push up your marks.

One major theme runs through all of the issues, and that is the idea of the sanctity of life. It is a central theme of all religious traditions, and is easier covered here as a reference section than in each Unit individually. Use the information from this double page to add to the details in other Units. Approach all the issues from the start point of how they are affected by an idea of sanctity, or how that idea affects them.

Look at the chart which follows, it gives you quotations from the major faiths about the sanctity of life. Can you write a paragraph to explain this attitude to life in each religion?

You will see that life is special and sacred to all religions, from its start to its end. Since it is special, we should show respect for it: respect for the embryo which may be changed genetically; for the child who needs a bone marrow transplant; for the man dying in agony of an incurable disease; for the addict trying to come off heroin; for the homeless man on the street corner; for the murderer who will die in prison. How much of that do you agree with?

Those issues can provoke strong reactions – you'll see that is a fact in some of the religious responses, and you'll feel it for yourself. One of the reasons for studying religions is so that we can understand their views, and so live more harmoniously. You might not agree, but you understand – it's a start. It will be important in the exam that you can show just that.

The Sanctity of Life as seen through Religious Teachings

BUDDHISM

Harm no living being (Precept)

The fifth element of the Noble Eightfold Path is *Right Livelihood*. This means having a job which causes no harm to any other being, and does not exploit any other being. In other words, respect for all life is required.

In a speech, the Dalai Lama said that *humans are all humans*. In other words, all the same.

ISLAM

He is the One who has created you all from a single soul. (Qur'an 7 v189)

Human beings should never kill animals, except for food. The Qur'an describes a sparrow at Judgement Day accusing a man of killing it for no reason, when killed in sport. The man is punished.

Do not take life – which Allah has made sacred – except for just cause. (Qur'an 17 v33)

CHRISTIANITY

Do not kill (Exodus 20 v 13)

Surely you know that you are God's temple and that God's spirit lives within you. (Corinthians 3 v16–17)

You (God) formed my inner most parts, you knitted me together in my mother's womb…your eyes saw my unformed substance; in your book were written all the days of my life, before I even had them. (Psalm 139 v13–16)

JUDAISM

I, and I alone am God…I kill and I give life… (Deuteronomy 32 v39)

It has been told you what is good and what the Lord wants of you; only to do justice and to love kindness and walk humbly with your God. (Micah 6 v8)

Do not kill (Exodus 20 v13)

When you (God) take away their breath, they die…when you give them breath, they are created; you give new life to the earth. (Psalm 104 v29–30)

HINDUISM

Hindus follow the principle of ahimsa – not harming others.

Harming others brings bad karma, which negatively affects future rebirths.

Do not do to another what you do not like to be done to yourself; that is the gist of the law – all other laws are variable. *(Mahabharata)*

SIKHISM

God sends us and we take birth. God calls us back and we die. (Adi Granth 1239)

Those who love God, love everybody. (Adi Granth 557)

This God is One…the Creator of all things. (Mul Mantra)

three

4 Religious Attitudes to Matters of Life

Introduction

This is the first of the *Contemporary Issues* topics. On the examination paper, it will be represented by one structured essay question. You choose to answer it – it isn't compulsory.

Matters of Life is a really interesting topic, because it is about the beginnings of life, and in particular, medical ethics related to *creating* and *shaping* life. It includes developments in medicine which have led to previously infertile couples being able to have children through artificial methods of conception. It also looks at such issues as genetic engineering, cloning, embryology, transplant surgery and blood transfusion. All of these have been, and still are, the cause of many arguments about whether they are ethically and/or morally right.

There are a number of fundamental questions linked to this topic. Try to keep them in mind as you work through it, thinking about how the ideas that come up relate to, or are affected by, the questions.

> when does life begin?
> conception...birth...some time in between

> do we exist before we physically exist?

> who is responsible for life?
> God...a couple...doctors...nature

Start to check the newspapers and news on a regular basis. If there are any stories which link to one of the Contemporary Issues topics, keep notes or the newspaper cutting. Putting these into your file in the right section of work expands the range of examples you can use, and often improves your ability to give moral or religious arguments. This is what the examiner wants to see.

Discuss these questions with a partner, or in small groups. The bubbles have ideas to help — have you any others? Can you see why different people would say the different answers?

Try to answer the following questions, justifying the answers you give. They are some of the questions which show the moral/ethical dilemma, caused by some of the advances we have made in our medical science. The fact is we have advanced to a state where what used to be dreamt of, now can be done — the question is whether it should be or not! Try them again when you have done the Unit.

1　Advances in medical science mean we can create, clone or genetically engineer life. Is this right, or is it unnatural, and are we playing God?

2　How might someone react to knowing they had been created or designed in a laboratory?

3　Is it ever right to do experiments on embryos, or are they sacred?

4　Is my body, including all of its components, totally mine to do with as I wish?

So, When Does Life Begin?

This is a key question. It helps people to decide whether they support or disagree with such things as genetic engineering. It also adds to the debate about artificial reproductive techniques, because if life starts at conception, should life start in a test-tube, or on a petri dish?

For each idea of when life begins, how does it affect the way we look at reproductive technologies, genetic engineering and cloning?

Some people say physical life is only a stage in our total existence – that we existed before this body and will exist after it. Our life is carried in a soul or spirit of some kind. This idea forms part of reincarnation theory, which states that we go through many lifetimes, each one affected by those which have gone before. The Eastern religious traditions such as Hinduism, Buddhism and Sikhism all share this view.

Is it creating something for a soul/spirit to go into?

Some people believe life begins at conception, for example, Roman Catholics. Many also believe conception should be natural. Buddhists believe the anatta (like the soul), takes its place at the instant the egg and sperm meet.

Some believe life begins at fourteen days, when the embryo attaches itself to the womb.

Is it when the heart begins to beat? That's at about three weeks.

Some say that at fourteen weeks, when the foetus begins to breathe for itself, then there is life.

Or is it when the first movements are felt – the quickening – at about nine weeks?

In the Old Testament, if a pregnant woman is assaulted and miscarries, she must be given compensation for that. If she dies, the aggressor should be executed. This makes the foetus quite distinct from life, and perhaps shows that life does not begin until the birth itself. It certainly shows that if there is a life before birth, that life has only limited rights, if any.

Others say that there is life when the foetus would be able to survive independently of the mother (with medical aid), which is at twenty-four weeks. This independence makes it a being in its own right.

So, what's the solution? Probably, quite a personal choice. Definitely it affects the decisions you make about that life.

four

The Rise of Medical Science

Medical science came on in leaps and bounds in the twentieth century, and shows no sign of slowing down in the twenty-first. We have moved from treating illnesses, to finding cures for the major illnesses of our time, and increasing life expectancy for all. Better hygiene and understanding of infection have increased the effectiveness of medical care. New advances such as blood transfusion, and transplant surgery have become common, with xenotransplantation now becoming a reality, as we use body parts from pigs genetically modified to be acceptable to the human system. No longer does nature decide who has children. Massive advances in fertility treatment mean a woman doesn't even need to have ever had sex to be able to conceive and have a child. The child she has can be *designed* in some ways, as the ability to genetically modify the foetus draws nearer.

The heartbreak and tragedy of a childless couple, who long for children of their own, can be overcome. A person whose own organs are failing and is suffering because of it, now has the opportunity of a *second chance*, even a *new life*, because of transplant surgery techniques. Where these operations were often affected by failure to find, or delay in finding, suitable matching organs for a patient, xenotransplantation may solve that problem. We can make copies of beings – remember Dolly the Sheep, she took nearly 300 attempts, but research is ongoing to improve that.

Where will medical science go next? Will we reach the point where you can go and select a child, and design it in every respect – looks, build, abilities, intelligence, even personality? What about a direct copy of someone – a perfect *Junior*? Do we really want to?

Mary Shelley wrote a book called 'Frankenstein' in 1818. The story described how a doctor, having built an adult human from body parts, gave it life. The resultant creature was a monster. Will science ever be able to make Shelley's story real?

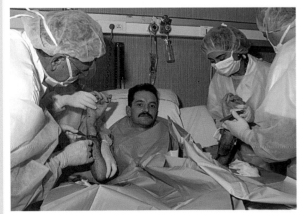

With a partner discuss the general ideas mentioned in this page. Do you think science is going too far? Has it already? If not, when will science have gone too far? Can we justify all this research?

In Medical Terms...

You need to have a basic knowledge of the range of artificial methods used by doctors to help infertile couples, and more recently, single women or lesbian couples, to have children. In the past, infertility has been an unchangeable, unfortunate fact, which couples had to accept. This is no longer the case. You also need to know what is meant by terms such as cloning, genetic engineering, transfusion and transplant. Cloning and genetic engineering have particular implications if we believe life begins at conception, or that life is sacred. Both involve tampering with life. Some would say they involve taking the place of God, or saying you know better than God because you want to change what has been created. Transfusion and transplant change what is natural. Is it right to interfere? Learn all these words, so that you can't be thrown by their appearance in the exam, and so that you can show off your knowledge. Begin a glossary, which will help with your revision later.

IVF

In vitro fertilisation. *In vitro* means *in glass*, and refers to the fact that the egg and sperm are collected and brought together in a petri dish. After a few days of incubation, conception has occurred and there are about eight identical cells (blastocyst). Several blastocysts are then placed into the woman's womb, to be monitored by doctors in the hope that a normal pregnancy will result. This method is used when the woman cannot naturally conceive. There is about a 25% success rate. The egg and sperm could have come from the couple and/or donors. The egg and sperm will have been kept frozen ready for implantation, and once fertilised any unused blastocysts must be destroyed within fourteen days.

AID/H

Artificial Insemination by Donor/Husband. Doctors collect several semen samples, which the man has produced by masturbating. These are artificially placed into the neck of the woman's womb when she ovulates. The hope is that fertilisation will occur. AIH is used when the husband has a low sperm count; AID when he has no sperm count (so a donor's sperm is needed), or he has a genetic disease he does not wish to pass on (this means his sperm are fertile, but the risk of transmission is too great). The success rate of this treatment is very low.

Others

There are a number of other methods, which are slight variations on those two. GIFT is a procedure in which the egg and sperm are collected and placed artificially into the woman's fallopian tube for fertilisation to occur there. ZIFT is where the egg and sperm, once collected, are allowed to fertilise before being put into the fallopian tubes for pregnancy to continue. ICSI involves injecting a single sperm into an egg, which is then transferred into the woman's womb. In any of these the sperm and/or egg could be from the couple or donor(s). There are different reasons to use each, which may indicate fertility problems in either/both partners.

Surrogacy

This is where another woman carries a pregnancy to full term for a couple. Conception is usually by artificial methods, and can be using the couple's and/or donor's egg and sperm. The resultant child is then brought up as the child of the couple. It is used in cases where the woman cannot medically carry a pregnancy. The surrogate will have agreed to bear the pregnancy. In the UK, although surrogacy occurs, it is illegal to pay someone to do it.

Think about it

1 If you can't naturally have children, shouldn't you accept it and get on with your life?

2 There are waiting lists for organ transplants, and not enough donors. Should it be legal to sell spare body parts, e.g. one of your two kidneys?

3 If sex is for reproduction, how can any method which doesn't involve sexual intercourse be right?

4 Should it be legal to pay people to provide reproductive services, such as eggs or sperm, or act as surrogates?

The Basics

①
Describe the various methods of artificial fertilisation/ reproduction available to couples who cannot have children naturally.

②
Explain the following terms – genetic engineering, cloning, blood transfusion, transplant surgery.

③
Reread the three fundamental questions on page 28. How might these affect attitudes to the scientific procedures mentioned here?

④
Why might some people believe that any advance in medical science should be welcomed, not rejected?

⑤
It is unnatural and wrong to have bits of machines or bits of other people in the place of your own body parts. Do you agree? Explain your answer.

four

Cloning (or human reproductive cloning)

This is the deliberate production of genetically identical human beings. This procedure is not legal in any country in the world. However, there is some work being done on cloning cells or body parts for use in transplant surgery (therapeutic cloning), which is generally considered acceptable in the medical community. This isn't regarded as creating life, though, which is why more people find it acceptable.

Genetic Engineering

This procedure modifies the genetic make-up of cells. There are now over 200 human gene therapy protocols, which can successfully treat genetic disorders, and get rid of certain genetic diseases. The Human Genome Project is trying to plot all 100,000 genes which make up humans. When this is complete, it may be possible to screen, prevent and treat all genetic disorders. Essentially, it changes the basic structure of the being and so alters what they will eventually be as humans. Some scientists have talked about finding the *gay gene* or the *criminal gene*. It isn't too big a step to suggest that, once found, it could be removed. Many are fearful of this potential abuse of genetic engineering, and so resist all of it.

Blood Transfusion

This is the use of blood products from other people to replace or boost blood in a patient. It is usually done as a result of blood loss, or as part of an operation. Blood given to a patient must match their own blood group, or their body rejects it, and they die.

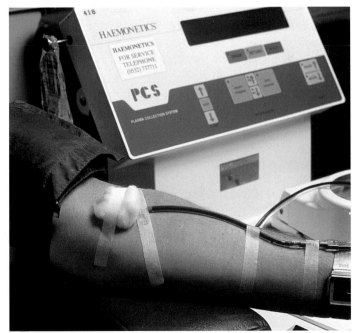

Transplantation

This is the procedure of replacing an organ in someone's body with the equivalent organ from someone else, usually someone who has died. It is done because their own organ does not work properly or at all. Recent advances have led to xenotransplantation, which is the use of organs from genetically modified animals. As with blood transfusion, the organ has to be accepted by the recipient's system, so there has to be a match.

In Religious Terms...

Let's concentrate on having children first...

To all religious traditions, life is sacred – a gift from God. Life belongs to God, and should be taken by God, because it has been given by Him. The sexual act is for reproduction, as well as being an expression of love between two people. God blesses marriages by giving children, each and every one of which God creates as an individual.

Following these beliefs, we can see that there may be concerns about science helping people to conceive.

How might someone who believes the above view fertility treatments? In these methods, who is giving life? — if not God, is it right? How do cloning and genetic engineering sit with these beliefs?

You can make general statements of what religious believers are likely to say, but you will need to know more clearly to attain the higher marks. Unfortunately, no holy book discusses these issues, so we have to look to statements about the sanctity of life, adultery and sex, and then apply them to the issues. The religious traditions provide guidance, based on their own interpretation of their holy books. It has to be remembered also that the desire, and *emotional need* to have a child often outweighs anything the religious tradition may say.

A Roman Catholic View

Catholicism believes that only married couples should have sex, because it is the union of the couple for the primary purpose of conceiving a child. Any sexual act outside of the bounds of a marriage is wrong in the eyes of the Church. This means that masturbation is wrong, because it is not part of the reproductive act. Life is sacred, and given by God to each of us individually (Genesis 1 v28 – *God created man and woman in his image*).

These ideas together mean that Catholicism does not support fertility treatments generally. First of all, AID/H and IVF require masturbation for the sperm to be produced, and most surrogate mothers conceive artificially so that the husband does not commit adultery. Secondly, conception should come from the union of a married couple – obviously, if a donor is involved, or if conception is not within the sexual act, this isn't the case. Where a donor is involved, it could be believed that a form of adultery had taken place. Thirdly, these methods point to the potential social and physical risks to the child. Perhaps the procedure will damage the embryo, perhaps the knowledge of being so conceived or having a donor as a father or a surrogate as a mother will prove too much for the child when it is older. In the same way, where a donor/surrogate was used, will the non-biological parent feel as close to the child as a natural parent would? Maybe the relationship will be damaged as a result. All told, Catholicism sees these treatments as playing God – God has decided a couple will not have children, and God's decision should be accepted, whether it can be understood or not.

Cloning and genetic engineering involve tampering with the DNA of an embryo, so are seen as a violation of the sanctity of life, as well as playing God. They also take away the idea of us each being created as unique individuals.

The Church of England View

There are a variety of views amongst church leaders. Montefiore, writing in 1959, said that using donated semen could be seen as breaking the marriage vows, and that the child growing up might find out and be hurt by the knowledge. However, he also said that you could consider the donated sperm as just a fertilising agent, nothing more. In this case, it would be acceptable, because there was no (adulterous) sexual act involved.

The general stance, set by the Synod, is that marriage is the ideal situation for conception and the upbringing of children. Children are God's blessing of a marriage. However, where a couple cannot conceive, medical science can help them. IVF and AIH/D are both acceptable, though any donors should not receive a payment. It can be seen that God is working through science, or has given us the medical knowledge.

The Church sees surrogacy as wrong. The natural mother might not wish to give the child up, or the child might find out. This is much more complicated than simple egg/sperm donation because the surrogate will have a bond with the child.

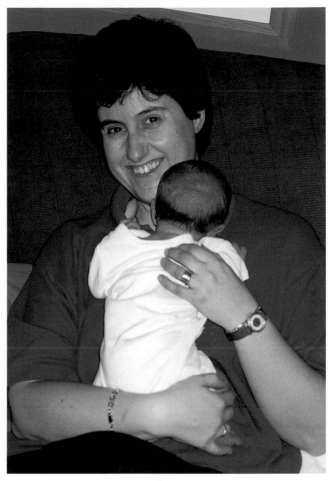

The Jewish View

Judaism has a range of ideas about this. Most Jews see masturbation as being completely wrong, which means that where semen has been acquired this way, it is unacceptable. Some rabbis believe that any fertilisation occuring outside the human body is unnatural, and therefore wrong.

Non-Orthodox Jews generally accept AIH. The semen may be a result of masturbation but it is for use in conception, so not *wasted seed*, which is against Jewish law. They don't generally accept AID because it is possible that the donor may be the unknowing father of several children. This could later lead to marriage between unknowing close blood relatives, which would break Jewish law. Jews share the idea with Christians that this is adultery.

The Basics

①
What are the major religious issues against using infertility treatments?

②
Outline the attitude to infertility treatment of two religious traditions.

③
Not every act of unprotected sex leads to a child, God chooses who will be blessed. AID/H and IVF do not guarantee children – this is God choosing again.
Do you agree? Explain your answer.

Decide for Yourself

For the following seven scenarios, if you were the one making the decision, would you allow treatment or not? In each case, explain why. For all, assume they are financially able to pay for treatment, and bring up children. For any couple, assume their relationship is strong and stable.

Next, use the two religious traditions you wrote about previously to construct advice for each scenario from those traditions. It should include explanations of what treatment they can/cannot have, and why.

Look at the following headlines. How would believers in the two religious traditions you have outlined view each story?

Womb to rent – surrogate mums

Surrogacy is wonderful, say parents of triplets

IVF – the gift of life?

We don't need men any more!

Babies can be grown in laboratories!

My two dads – biological and nurturing

Picking Out the Issues

You have seen that there are many issues involved in deciding to use fertility treatments. Religious and non-religious people share reasons, as well as having differing ones, to support or condemn this way of conceiving. Read the statements below. Make lists to show the two sides of the argument. Highlight those which are clearly religious.

My husband and I have been trying for children for twelve years. We have had tests and know it is not possible. The chance to use IVF could give us the gift of the child we have longed for, and which would make our lives complete. We can afford to give this child everything it needs, both financially and emotionally. Why should we not use medical science to help us?

Children belong in a family with a mum and dad. These treatments will let people other than that have children.

Where does medical knowledge come from, if not God? God gives us this knowledge, so that we can help each other, which is a duty for all. Surely then IVF etc should be embraced, not rejected.

God creates each of us individually, he decides what we will be. He is the sole creator of life — the only one.

There is nothing natural about test tubes and injections. Children come from the most natural act there is — they should be born, not built.

IVF is expensive — money talks, and makes everything unfair. If everyone had the same chance, I'd find it okay, but most people can't afford this.

Genetic engineering will one day help us to eradicate many diseases. That has to be good.

Go back through the details of how religious traditions view these methods. Can you add any more reasons to your lists?

Use these lists to make up a conversation exploring the issue of medicine supporting conception.

four

Transfusions and Transplants

What do you know? Check back to page 33 to find a short explanation of each.

In 1905, the first transplant procedure – corneal grafting – took place. The first organ transplant was done in 1954. Today transplants are commonplace. *What can be transplanted?* Most organs come from the bodies of people who agreed to donate them before they died, or relatives of the deceased agreeing to donate organs. Some come from living people, e.g. one of their two kidneys, bone marrow etc. There is a shortage of most major organs for donation. *Why do you think this is the case?*

Blood transfusion dates back to 1818. At first, it was very risky because blood group matching only began in 1900. Blood products, gained from donations, are vital to the running of hospitals, as they are used in all operations. The demand for blood from hospitals is constant and as such campaigns are regularly run to encourage more people to give blood.

More people are happier to give blood than to donate organs after their death. *Why do you think this is so?*

NHS Organ Donor Register
donorcard
I want to help others to live in the event of my death

Read the following conversation, and pick out the arguments for and against organ donation.

> Picked up one of those donor cards the other day.

> Really? Gives me the creeps to think I'll get cut up and distributed when I'm dead.

> No, it's important. I don't need my body if I'm dead, do I? Bits of me might actually save someone's life. It's comforting to think that my last acts can be so valuable and important. You could say that I am still alive in a way.

> Yes, but it's not respectful to cut someone up after they've died. If my child died, I'd want to hold them and remember what they were, not decide if the doctors can whisk them away and chop them up.

> It must be very difficult to make that decision, that's why I've decided for myself.

> Now they are genetically changing animals so that they can grow organs which can be transplanted into people. I don't like that either — it isn't natural.

> There are so many people who need such help, anything they can do like that must be good.

> At the end of the day, I think transplantation oversteps the mark of where God is. If that means someone has to be blind, that's God's call. If someone will die, again its God's call.

> Got to disagree with you there. If there's a God, he's given us this knowledge. We should use it.

Read the next page, and make notes about the attitude of two traditions.

The Christian Attitude

No mainstream Christian tradition has a problem with either blood transfusion, donation from living donors, or donation after death where consent has been given.

It can be seen as an act of love in each case, either to a relative or a stranger. Jesus' central message was one of love, *Love your neighbour* (Mark 12 v33). Donation without consent shows no respect to the deceased or their body. In Catholic terms, you can sacrifice a part for the good of the whole, so a person donating organs, tissue or blood does so to help others, which is acceptable. No Christian group agrees with transplantation from embryos, as they believe this desecrates life.

The Muslim View

Whoever saves a life, it would be as if he saved the life of all the people (Qur'an). Clearly, Muslims should be able to donate organs because this helps others. However, it is against Muslim law to mutilate a dead body, which would forbid any donation after death. These donations are the most important, because they are the major organs – heart, lungs, liver etc. Two Shariah rules solve the dilemma – first, when need overrules prohibition (so the live person's need outweighs the rule of not mutilating the dead) and second, that you choose the lesser of two evils in any situation (so saving a life by breaking a rule is a lesser evil than letting someone else die for want of the organ).

Regarding the use of foetal tissue, Islam is quite clear. Where the tissue comes from a miscarried foetus, or lawful abortion (one performed to save the mother's life), it can be used. Otherwise, it does not demonstrate that life is sacred and God-given.

The Jewish View

Jews face a similar, if not greater, dilemma than Muslims face. An overriding Jewish obligation is to preserve human life, which transplantation does. However, not only is it forbidden to mutilate a body, but also the whole of the body should be buried.

Most Jewish authorities allow a transplant which is likely to save a life, following the Talmudic principle that *one party is helped and the other not harmed*. Some say that when an organ has been transplanted, it is no longer a part of the deceased, so there is no problem with the burial. Having said that, heart transplants are not supported, because there is not enough time between certified death and removal to meet Jewish law, which means the organ removal contributes to the death – illegal in Jewish law.

Many rabbis have said it is a religious obligation to help others whilst alive, so if you can donate without being harmed, then you should.

four

Exam Tips

In the exam, you have to be able to pick out exactly what questions are asking. The second part of the paper is made up of *structured essay questions* (questions linked to one theme). You can't afford to misread these, because each is worth twenty marks - a quarter of the total for the paper.

Let's look at some questions and answers. *Read the question, and break it into bits. Then read the answer – does it cover the bits?*

1   Explain what is meant by AID, and why it is used. (5)

Answer – it is a form of artificial help for a couple who can't conceive. The doctors take sperm and inject it into the woman's womb when she ovulates. They hope it will fertilise the egg, and a pregnancy will develop.

2   Explain what is meant by organ donation, and the relevance of religious beliefs to this issue. (10)

Answer – this is the donation of organs by someone, either after death (e.g. heart), or whilst alive (e.g. one of your two kidneys). The organ is given to a patient who has either no such organ, or one which is so faulty it is useless. It can save their life. Many people carry donor cards, because the organs have to be removed as soon as they die, or they are useless. Nowadays, even whole arms or legs can be transplanted.

Religious beliefs have an impact on this issue, because they either encourage or discourage people to donate. If your religion said you can't donate, you wouldn't. For Christians, there isn't a problem, as long as there was consent. It is seen as an act of love – Love your neighbour, as Jesus said. They could point to the fact that they are part of a whole community, so the Principle of Totality (one bit sacrificed for the good of the whole) comes in. Muslims would agree with organ donation. They aren't supposed to mutilate dead bodies, but must meet a need if they can. Where someone needs an organ, it is acceptable. The Qur'an says that Muslims must save a life if they can. Organ donation does that.

Neither answer would get the full marks, (shown in brackets) although the answer to question 2 is much better than the one to question 1. Each has two distinct parts – the explanation, then an extra bit. Don't lose sight of these two parts. In the second question, you've met one of the many ways to say what do two religious traditions think about x? Get used to the different ways, so you don't get flustered in the exam.

Choose any topic within this Unit, and substitute it for AID and organ donation in those questions. Now write full mark answers.

5 Religious Attitudes to Matters of Death

What is Death?

When I am dead

by Christina Rossetti

When I am dead, my dearest,
Sing no sad songs for me;
Plant thou no roses at my head,
Nor shady cypress tree.
Be the green grass above me
With showers and dewdrops wet;
And if thou wilt, remember,
And if thou wilt, forget.

I shall not see the shadows,
I shall not feel the rain;
I shall not hear the nightingale
Sing on, as if in pain:
And dreaming through the twilight
That doth not rise nor set,
Haply I may remember,
And haply may forget.

After death

by Christina Rossetti

The curtains were half drawn, the floor was swept
And strewn with rushes, rosemary and may
Lay thick upon the bed on which I lay,
Where thro' the lattice ivy-shadows crept.
He leaned above me, thinking that I slept
And could not hear him, but I heard him say:
'Poor child, poor child': and as he turned away
Came a deep silence, and I knew he wept.
He did not touch the shroud, or raise the fold
That hid my face, or take my hand in his
Or ruffle the smooth pillows for my head;
He did not love me living; but once dead
He pitied me; and very sweet it is
To know he still is warm tho' I am cold.

Read these two poems. They suggest a conscious being still exists after the death of the body.

What is your idea about what happens to us after the death of our body? Does anything happen? Why do you think people want there to be something more than just this life?

All religions talk about life after death. They link it to rewards and punishments, to the triumph of good over evil. How do these ideas fit with yours?

This Unit looks at attitudes to death. These attitudes impact upon our acceptance or rejection of such practices as euthanasia and suicide. They are closely linked to the value we give to life itself – its sanctity. That leads us to consider treatment of the terminally ill (palliative care), and of the elderly. You will meet all of these, from the view of the religious traditions in this Unit.

Before you continue, with a partner, discuss your attitude to these four elements — euthanasia, suicide, palliative care, care of the elderly.

(Life after) Death

It can only be possible to talk about what may or may not count as life after death, if we first have a definition of *death*. Is it when we stop breathing? What about when there is no brain stem activity? What about someone on life support, with no hope of recovery – are they dead yet?

'Death is the final cessation of vital functions', according to the Oxford Reference Dictionary.

Some traditions believe that death occurs after the soul has left the body, and that this happens at some time after the vital organs have stopped functioning.

Several religious traditions believe that after death, our soul will become aware again when it is awakened for Judgement Day. Then it is sent to heaven or hell, depending upon the actions of the person in their lifetime. Christians, Jews and Muslims share this belief. There is belief in a physical resurrection – that we will be awakened as our physical bodies. Catholics also believe that after death, the soul goes to purgatory, where the prayers of the living could cleanse it for the Judgement Day. Many Christian groups believe you have to have been baptised/confirmed to go to heaven.

Other religious traditions believe that our soul lives through many lifetimes. Every word, thought and action contributes to making the next lifetime better or worse. Each lifetime our soul gains the chance to become wiser, or purer. Eventually through wisdom and purity, our soul is no longer tied to being reborn in this way, and attains a form of heaven, Nirvana. Buddhists, Hindus and Sikhs share versions of this general idea.

Look at the images and discuss the questions.

Do resurrected bodies get old and die?

Is it fair for hell to be forever?

Is hell oblivion?

Do any of these make up for the suffering and evil of our world?

So, is it a case of what goes around, comes around?

Stories to control people, or good guesses of the future?

To Whom Does Life Belong?

It might seem very clear – my body, my right to decide. But…

Your parent/guardian makes major decisions for you before you reach sixteen. For example, they have to give consent for any operation. You can't marry before eighteen without their consent. You aren't legally allowed to drive until you are seventeen, drink until eighteen. There are many impositions on our lives, which suggest someone else has control.

What About Life Itself?

You couldn't help someone to kill themselves, even if you could demonstrate that had been their wish. It used to be illegal to try to kill yourself. Many religious leaders will not lead services for those who have killed themselves, or let their bodies be buried in church graveyards.

All that suggests that life itself isn't quite your own. So, whose is it?

Clearly, God decides who lives and who dies. As the Creator, God owns us, and our lives are sacred.

Check back to pages 26–7. What does this mean for euthanasia or suicide?

Religious traditions state that when dealing with life at its beginning or end, we have to be aware that that life belongs to God. It should be treated with the utmost respect, and not wasted. We should take care not to make decisions which only God is entitled to make. If we play God, we will have to face the consequences in the next life.

How will a belief in afterlife affect behaviour in this case?

> *When you (God) take away their breath, they die…when you give them breath, they are created; you give new life to the earth.*
>
> Psalm 104 v29–30

> *God sends us and we take birth, God calls us back, and we die*
>
> Adi Granth 1239

> *I, and I alone, am God…I kill and I give life*
>
> Deuteronomy 32 v39

> *So God created man in his image*
>
> Genesis 1 v27

> *It is Allah who gives life and death*
>
> Qur'an 40 v67

Organisation Profile

The Christian Medical Fellowship (CMF)

The CMF is a Christian doctors organisation. All doctors take the Hippocratic Oath, which says life is sacred, and should be protected; CMF doctors additionally follow Christian teachings. This includes not supporting euthanasia, and treating the matters met in the previous Unit with great caution. Check out their website *www.cmf.org.uk* to read their views on matters of life and death.

The Basics

①
What is the religious attitude to life? Use quotes to support your answer.

②
Describe the beliefs of two faiths about life after death.

③
Define death.

④
Death is not the end, just a step.
Do you agree?
Explain your answer.

Suicide

Fact File

- In the UK and Ireland, there is one suicide every 79 minutes.

- There were 6,216 suicides in the UK in 1999.

- About 20% of those who attempt suicide try again.

- 76% of suicides are by men.

- There has been an 8% decrease in the rate of suicide in England since 1990, but the rate overall for UK and Ireland has gone up.

- There are over 142,000 cases of attempted suicide each year, based on hospital treatment figures.

Suicide in the Law

Before 1961, it was illegal to commit suicide – figure that one out! It is still illegal to help someone to commit suicide, though. The Suicide Act (1961) states that *a person who encourages, assists or gets someone else to assist another in attempting suicide will, if convicted, face a maximum sentence of 14 years imprisonment.* So, the law values life highly. Of course, a prosecution would only take place if there was enough evidence of the crime, and if such a prosecution was in the public interest. This means fewer cases go to court than you might expect. However, it is under this law that a number of people have been convicted when they've helped their partner/spouse to die (euthanasia).

Suicide is the deliberate and direct act of taking one's own life. How do the religious traditions view it?

Read the Fact File. Does anything surprise you?

With a partner, try to explore the reasons, which cause people to try to kill themselves, and what it is that drives them to this action. Are they very brave? Or taking an easy way out?

By committing suicide, what are people saying about the value of their life?

Religious traditions claim our lives belong to God. Is suicide likely to be acceptable to religious groups? Why? What effect might that have on religious believers in despair?

Organisation Profile

The Samaritans *(www.samaritans.org.uk)* was set up in 1953 by Chad Varah, a Church of England vicar in London. His organisation started as himself counselling people, whilst volunteers did everything else. Seeing the impact that these volunteers had in their role of befrienders, he realised that many people's despair and suicidal feelings could be alleviated by just talking to someone, and being accepted without prejudice. This is a basic value of the Samaritan movement. Varah set up The Samaritans, and its success is available for all to see.

The Samaritans want to see suicide figures decrease, and a society where people can explore and express their feelings, and be acknowledged and respected by others for them. Their beliefs are based on these values – that it is important to be able to explore those feelings, that being listened to helps, and that everyone has the right to make  fundamental decisions about their life, including to die by suicide.

Christians and Suicide

Your body is a temple to God. (1 Corinthians 3)

When you (God) take away their breath, they die (Psalm 104 v.29)

All Christian traditions believe suicide is wrong – a grave sin. Christians believe that life belongs to God, and is entrusted to us, so that we can serve God on earth. When you consider suicide, it is wrong because you are saying you know better than God, you are making the decision to end your life. You reject God's love for you, by saying you aren't worthy of life. You reject God, because you were created in God's image, which you are destroying. You are saying those who love you are better off without you, even though suicide has the longest impact on relatives and friends compared to any other form of dying.

Many vicars and priests will neither carry out a service, nor allow burial in consecrated land for those who died by suicide. However, they will try to give the family as much support as they can.

In the twentieth century, attitudes to suicide changed from seeing it as a criminal, even selfish act, to seeing it as a sign of immense distress. This has affected the way that attempted suicides, and relatives of suicide victims, have been supported by their faith communities. There is much more understanding and compassion shown, particularly through befriending ministries.

Buddhism and Suicide

When the karmic force of past deeds reaches maturity, a person experiences ... unpleasurable mental states. They are but a natural consequence of his own previous actions. The Dalai Lama.

Buddhism believes in reincarnation, which is that our ever-changing spirit goes through many lifetimes in the cycle of rebirth. The rebirth we have is dependent upon our words, thoughts and actions in previous lives. We should try to cultivate good karma through positive living, which will shape our rebirth. Those who are in despair of their lives need our support and compassion – back to the idea of befriending. Their suffering is actually a result of their own karma, from this or a previous lifetime, and must be worked through. Buddhists believe that if a person commits suicide, then their spirit may become trapped between lives, as their distress trapped them in the actual experience of death. In imagery, this is shown as a kind of hell state. Their spirit cannot move on through the process of rebirth, and when it eventually does, it will be into a negative rebirth, as they have created more bad karma.

five

Islam and Suicide

Nor kill nor destroy yourself (Qur'an 4 v29)

A man was inflicted with wounds and he committed suicide and so Allah said : My slave has caused death on himself hurriedly, so I forbid Paradise for him. (Hadith)

Islam's attitude to suicide, then, is very clear – it is wrong. Actually, it comes into a category of crime so wrong that it is believed the soul of the suicide victim will be sent to hell by Allah, where it will be severely punished. It is labelled in Islamic law as the act of a coward.

Why is it so wrong? Life is absolutely sacred in Islam, and the taking of a life is seen as representative of taking the life of all humans. In opposition to this, saving one life is valued as saving the life of everyone. Allah created each of us individually, and values each of us highly – we belong to Allah.

First female suicide bomber

Committing suicide brings much shame onto a family, and this may affect them in their standing in the community – both how others view them as well as their own self identity. Those who attempt suicide would face condemnation, as well as some compassion.

'My duty is to fight for my religion and family. I go to Paradise' – the last speech of the latest suicide bomber

The issue of *suicide bombers* is very real in the world today. Many Muslims say this is against Allah, especially in such cases as the American Twin Towers (11-09-2001), because there are so many innocent victims, including Muslims. In the case of Palestine, suicide bombing is less condemned because the victims are seen as part of a whole nation, and Israel and its people are considered guilty of crimes against Islam. Suicide bombers are seen as martyrs, who are sacrificing their souls for the sake of their faith and nation, so their act is one of resistance, and the intention is not simply to kill themselves. The suicide bombers are held up as heroes, and their families become celebrated in their communities. It is said they will go to Paradise, as will their families.

Muslims denounce Twin Towers assault as un-Islamic

The Basics

① Define *suicide*.

② Explain the attitudes of two religious traditions to suicide. Use quotations as support, from pages 26–7 as well as this Unit.

③ Describe the values and work of the Samaritans.

④ Would you expect to see religious believers working for Samaritan-type agencies given the belief of their faiths that suicide is wrong, even a crime against God? Explain your answer.

⑤ *Religions are supposed to help those in need. Those who commit suicide, or try to, obviously have a need. Religious people should help them and their families, not turn them away.* How far do you agree? Give reasons and explain your answer.

Euthanasia

This is defined as a *gentle death* or *mercy killing*. However, you need to know a fuller definition for the examination. Euthanasia is the taking of a life with a compassionate intention in order to end suffering. The person being euthanised could be suffering from a painful and incurable disease, such as liver cancer, or the victim of a degenerative disease, which is robbing them of all quality of life, or on life support with no hope of recovery.

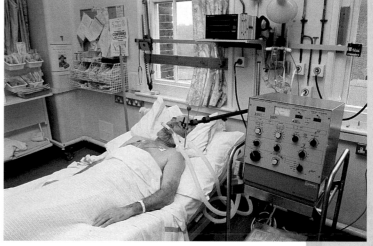

Euthanasia is illegal in Britain, being seen at best as breaking the Suicide Act 1961, which forbids anyone from helping someone else to die and carries a fourteen year jail sentence. It can be viewed as manslaughter, or at worst, murder, which carries a life sentence. Doctors do switch off life support machines when patients have no sign of brain activity, and they do administer drugs to ease pain, which also shorten life. Neither of these is seen as euthanasia in the UK.

Euthanasia has a long history. Hippocrates, a Greek doctor, openly stated he would not prescribe drugs to help someone end their life. His stance has become the Hippocratic Oath, sworn by doctors in the UK. In 1516 CE, Thomas More defended euthanasia as the last treatment option for doctors to give, if the patient wanted it. In the twentieth century, in most western countries, groups exist to try to make euthanasia legal. In some countries, it is legal. The debate rages on.

Types of Euthanasia

Euthanasia can be split into *active* and *passive*. Active euthanasia is where something is done, perhaps a drug administered, to end a person's life. Passive is where the medication they are on is withdrawn, and they die naturally, but sooner. It can also be split into *voluntary* and *involuntary*. Voluntary euthanasia is where the patient has asked to be helped to die, so they have given their full consent to the act. Involuntary is where the patient is helped to die, but has been unable to give consent, for example if they are on life support (their family has given consent).

> I will give no deadly medicine to anyone if asked, nor suggest such counsel, and in like manner I will not give to a woman a pessary to produce abortion.
>
> Hippocratic Oath

The Basics

Use the information from these pages, and pages 26–7 to help you.

① Define euthanasia, including its types.

② Give reasons why people support or condemn euthanasia.

③ Explain the legal attitude to euthanasia in the UK.

④ Describe a system where euthanasia is legal.

⑤ Describe the work and aims of the Voluntary Euthanasia Society.

Talking Euthanasia

> Have you seen the Diane Pretty case? She lost her legal fight for euthanasia.

> Yes, Annie Lindsell won hers a few years ago. The Judges said her doctor could give her medication, even though it would kill her. She had a degenerative disease, and had had enough.

> I'm glad in a way, because I don't think doctors should take life — they should save it. Maybe it's time to die when God decides, not doctors — you know, nature.

> What if God works through doctors, and it is God deciding? He gave them the knowledge, after all. Life is very special, though, can't be taken just like that.

> Makes me worry, too. If we said euthanasia was legal, how would it be kept proper? I think people would abuse it — get rid of rich relatives, or embarrassing ones. It's a slippery slope.

> Well, it is legal in the Netherlands, and the system isn't abused there. I wouldn't want to suffer like some people do, I'd want to say enough is enough. We give our pets the right not to suffer. Why can't we have that right?

Read the conversation. Make a list of reasons for and against euthanasia. Add any of your own. Take each reason and develop it by explaining it, and maybe giving a made-up example.

Euthanasia is legal in the Netherlands. It has been legal since 1981, with current recording and reporting procedures in place since 1993. There are strict guidelines governing its practice –

- the patient must be suffering unbearably.

- their desire to die and their suffering must be lasting.

- their decision must have been voluntary and informed, and they must clearly and correctly understand the future of their illness.

- the patient must decide they want no other solution. The time and manner of death must not cause misery to them or others.

- a specified number of different professionals must have been involved throughout, and a medical doctor must inform the choice of, and prescription of, drugs.

The system is designed to help the sufferers and their families to keep the process medically controlled and appropriate, and to prevent abuse.

Go through this paragraph. How does each element guard against abuse, or misuse by sufferers, or anyone else?

Organisation Profile

The Voluntary Euthanasia Society was set up in 1935. Its aim is to make it legal for competent adults to receive medical help and die at their own persistent and considered request, if they have incurable and painful conditions. They want to legalise assisted dying, under strict procedures.

Find out about this organisation, and the whole debate at *www.ves.org.uk*.

In Religious Terms...

Check back to the religious attitudes to suicide (pages 45–6). They contribute much to this debate, since euthanasia can be seen as suicide, one step removed.

The Roman Catholic View

Roman Catholics are absolute moralists, following the Ten Commandments, which include 'Do not kill'. The Magisterium denounced euthanasia both as morally and criminally wrong.

Do Catholics agree with euthanasia?

The R C Church points out that life is sacred, given by God and taken by God – when God decides.

Does euthanasia go against any of these points? How?

They claim that making an attempt on the life of an innocent person opposes God's love for that person, because they are not worthy of life.

They say that everyone has a duty, and it is part of God's plan.

Could euthanasia be a show of love? Explain.

The Church believes that the request to die is really a cry for attention, and that with adequate palliative care, people would not seek euthanasia. It is up to society to look after people properly.

What does euthanasia do to the plan?

The Dutch Protestant Church Stance

Their acceptance of euthanasia is almost unique in Christianity. It is probably a result of changes within the law, but they interpret differently ideas that Roman Catholics use. Read on, but try to interpret ideas as accepting of euthanasia.

Is life sacred?

The Dutch Protestant Stance feels that God creates us all individually. Suffering can make life undignified, which makes us and our families suffer more. God loves us, so does not want us to suffer.

What does this say about their attitude to euthanasia and the quality of life?

God has given us the medical knowledge and ability to care for patients wisely. That care includes the mind and soul of the person, which can be affected by extreme suffering.

Where euthanasia is not legal, people can feel forced to commit suicide – if they are able to. Those people have to be alone when they die, and must have kept their intention secret, or those people could be charged with crimes. Loved ones who help them can be charged. Often their church will prohibit them from services or burial. All of this causes immense distress for the sufferer, their friends and family. The DPC felt that as Christians, they had to be compassionate, and should respect the fact that in some cases a quicker death that is natural is better, even loving. The Church holds services at the death and after, and allows burials.

Does this allow the use of medicine to end life?

five

The Islamic Stance

Euthanasia is forbidden in Islam. Allah gives and takes life. Anyone asking for euthanasia, or carrying out euthanasia will be guilty of a great crime against man and God, and will be punished in hell after this life. It is just the same as suicide for the one requesting it, or murder for the one carrying it out. Murder carries the death penalty.

Muslims believe that the lives of every one of us are planned out to the tiniest detail by Allah – from birth to death.

How does euthanasia go against this?

Allah's plan for us is broken by euthanasia, because things may happen to us for the benefit of others, even dying in this way.

How could this be so?

We are Allah's creation, and cannot hope to understand why He allows the sufferings of some. We should not then take matters into our own hands, but should accept the will of Allah.

How does euthanasia go against this?

Muslims believe we should care for the dying in a way that helps them, not kills them.

The Buddhist Stance

Check back to the Buddhist stance on suicide (page 45) – it is forbidden, and causes greater harm than good. Similarly, euthanasia is seen to be wrong. Even if someone feels that what they are doing is compassionate, and a form of help, in fact, it is not. It shortens the time left for a person who is working through past bad karma. They will only have to work through it again.

Buddhist monks will include meditation on death in their training, as it is inevitable, and an example of the temporary nature of all things. There are many books written about facing death and dying, for example, *The Tibetan Book of Living and Dying*. In these books there is no place for euthanasia, only palliative care.

The Basics

① Go back to the section about suicide. Research two traditions' attitudes. Now, using that information, alongside this on euthanasia, explain two religious attitudes to euthanasia.

② The Principle of Double Effect is that one action may be carried out with a specific intention, yet have a secondary result. Roman Catholics accept the use of medication in this way as a valid treatment of the terminally ill. Can we say this is the most appropriate use of a doctor's skills and training?

③ *There is nothing sacred about the last weeks of a terminal, painful illness.* Do you agree? Give reasons and explain your answer, showing more than one point of view.

④ *Euthanasia, quite simply, is murder.* Do you agree? Give reasons and explain your answer, showing more than one point of view.

The Hospice Movement

A hospice is a hospital for the dying.

Originally, hospices were places for travellers, the sick and the needy to stay. They were a part of monasteries – set up by Christians. Over time, some of them began to specialise in looking after the dying.

When people are dying, they have special medical needs, but these aren't their only needs. They also have spiritual and psychological needs. Many dying people can not express the true pain of their suffering, or the difficulties they find in even simple tasks. They don't want to let their families see the reality – for they will suffer more than they are doing. They often feel a burden, and a nuisance. In hospices, they get the medical care that they need, but they also get more spiritual and psychological care. They allow themselves to be ill. The burdens they feel are not so great.

When someone is dying, they can't be cured – only cared for. If that care covers all aspects of their being, they will not wish for euthanasia. This is the basic idea of hospices. There are more people working in the hospice to be able to cover all aspects of every patient's needs.

The Aims of Hospices

Firstly, to relieve physical symptoms of illness. In other words, to get rid of as much pain as is possible. This includes whatever it takes - massage, meditation, and relaxation. Secondly, to care for the emotional and spiritual wellbeing of the patient. Many dying people have unfinished business, which is a worry to them – the hospices help them to sort things out. Many patients are angry – 'why me?' – and the hospices help them to come to terms with their fate. Many patients need to be listened to, and given time – relatives often can't cope with this, but the hospices do. Thirdly, to support the families of patients – they suffer too. Hospices provide many support networks and services for the family, even after the death of the patient. Lastly, to educate others caring for the dying, and to work out new, better ways to care for them – invaluable in the future, so that the experience built up in hospices can be used in other places.

Religious groups point to hospices as the way forward for terminally ill people. God wants us to care for these people, to look after them, to express God's love for them, not to kill them.

The Basics

① Explain the role and aims of hospices.

② Find out about the work of a hospice near you, possibly from the Internet. Write an article about it.

five

Caring for the Elderly

In Western cultures, there has been a proliferation of homes for the elderly. Western culture is based upon the nuclear family – mum, dad and their kids – and other relatives don't figure in that. It is quite unusual to find the grandparents generation sharing a house with their children's families. It isn't to say we don't care about our parents when they grow old, we just don't seem to want them in our houses.

Do you agree?

As people grow older, they can have more fulfilling lives, and want their independence longer. At the same time, that ageing process means people are even older, and so more fragile and need more care.

What are the factors affecting whether people welcome their ageing parents into their homes to live? Would you welcome that prospect? Explain why/why not.

In some cultures, it is expected that people will look after their parents when they get old. This is certainly true in developing countries, for example. It is also true for certain religious traditions, such as Islam.

If you lived in such a culture, do you think you would welcome your parents into your home? What are the benefits of such a system?

Arguments for taking/not taking relatives in include space, arguments, too needy (all against), and repaying their bringing you up, duty, extra help, compassion, friendship (all for).

Do you think that the general way our society treats the elderly is why we choose to find reasons why not, rather than reasons for? Explain your ideas.

The Basics

①

How can the elderly be cared for by society?

②

Why do some families welcome aged relatives into their homes? Why do some not?

③

Explain the attitude of two religious traditions to the care of the elderly.

④

Having given to us, we should give back to them. Do you agree with this attitude to the elderly? Give reasons for your answer.

If any of these were your ageing relatives, would you take them in to live at your house? Imagine you are married with two children. For each relative, make a list of the benefits and hazards of them coming to live with you. Which one(s) would you definitely take/not take? Justify those decisions.

Aged 90, has Alzheimer's Disease, so is confused and needs a lot of care. Carer available.

Aged 85, very active until a stroke two years ago, which took strength from one side of the body. Very strict with you as a child.

Aged 80, still active, always visiting friends and is involved in local community – sees themselves as retired but not useless so quite independent.

Aged 79, heavy smoker, with bad cough, is very helpful, fussing around the house and children all the time.

Aged 84, doing a couple of GCSEs at a local night school. Likes organising people, and is active in the local church and choir

In Religious Traditions

Christianity

Honour your father and mother (Exodus 20 v12)

The Old Testament gives us this clear instruction, and it can be interpreted in many ways – so long as our parents are looked after, and can live dignified lives, we fulfil the commandment. Christians recognise that old age is a time of vulnerability and insecurity, and support is needed for the aged. However, it isn't a Christian tradition to have the aged in our homes, rather the tradition is for them to have their independence as long as possible, with the support of their families, and then move into a nursing home. In fact, care in a nursing home can be better than any family could provide, especially if the old person has specific medical needs. In this case, the commandment is better met by such a placement.

Islam

Show kindness to both your parents (Qur'an 17 v23)

May his nose be rubbed in dust who found his parents, one or both, approaching old age and did not enter Paradise by serving them

He who…does not acknowledge the honour due to our elders is not one of us.

Islam is an extended family society, and care of elderly members of the family is part of that culture. It is common for older family members to live with other generations, though it is they who have taken the younger members in, and not vice versa. If a Muslim does not fulfil this duty of looking after parents, Allah will make him or her suffer in the afterlife. Old people are seen as a source of wisdom and experience, and given great respect, not a burden to be sent somewhere else.

Hinduism

Hindus follow five religious duties, which must be met daily, and which help to develop a sense of service towards others. One of these duties is Pitri Yajna – service and care of parents and the elderly. Just as parents brought up and provided for their children, so the reverse becomes a duty when the children are old enough. They should also show respect, continue to obey their parents' wishes and seek their parents' advice on matters. Many Hindu families are large, and so it would be impossible for the parents to live with all of their children. In this case, it is usually the eldest son who has this particular duty.

Sikhism

When a man acts in a morally irresponsible manner towards his parents his religious acts and worship are futile.

Sikhism is similar to Hinduism and Islam in its attitude to care of the elderly. They are looked after within the home of one of their children – the extended family culture. Sewa (service to others) is a duty of Sikhs. Gurdwaras act as day care centres for the elderly in the community, sharing the families' burdens.

five

Exam Tips

The AO2 Questions

There are three types of questions on the paper. You've already met the evaluative ones, now let's look at the ones where you apply your knowledge. They are marked using a Levels of Response style system, which means you have to give breadth and depth to your answer to get near to the top grades. Breadth in an answer is when you give a range of reasons, or comments to support what you are saying. Depth in an answer is when you give explanations to each of the points you have made. The more explanation, the greater the depth.

On the sample paper, which you can find in the back of this book (page 104), you can see that the middle part of each B question is worth ten marks. It actually asks for quite a lot, but in a very concise way. Maybe the actual examinations will change from this format, but let's work out how to answer that one.

How might religious teachings and beliefs influence a person about euthanasia?

To answer this, you first need to show you know what euthanasia actually is. Learn a good definition, with a couple of examples.

Next, remember that the syllabus asks you to be aware of the teachings of two religious traditions about all of the topics. So you'll have to be able to say what two lots of religious believers think. Be able to give some teachings – general statements – to pin your comments to. If you can only be vague, then you'll limit yourself to the lower range of marks.

Try to answer that question. Use the Levels of Response table below to help improve the quality of your answer. You could try to write an answer for each level. When you've done that, swap suicide or care for the elderly for euthanasia, and answer the question again.

Table for Levels of Response (AO1 and AO2)

LEVEL	CRITERIA	EXAMPLE
LEVEL ONE	Relevant statement of information or explanation which is limited in scope or content.	Roman Catholics believe abortion is wrong, because it says 'Do not kill'.
LEVEL TWO	Relevant but basic information, analysis or explanation presented in a structured way. Could be several reasons/ points.	Roman Catholics follow the Bible which teaches that it is wrong to kill. Abortion can be classed as killing, so it is wrong.
LEVEL THREE	A sound analysis or explanation presented in an organised way.	As level two, but more than one reason/point used.
LEVEL FOUR	A comprehensive, clear and coherent response showing awareness of and insight into the relevance and/or application of religious facts, ideas and/or attitudes.	Several reasons/points, usually with examples and using quotes. There is depth and breadth to this answer.

6 Religious Attitudes to Drug Abuse

Introduction

What Drugs do you Know the Names of?

List them. Did you know they come into four broad categories? There are stimulants, depressants, hallucinogens, and opoid analgesics.

Stimulants (uppers) work by acting on your central nervous system, and increase the activity of your brain. Depressants (downers) do exactly the opposite, they work on your central nervous system, and slow down the brain activity. Hallucinogens act on your mind, distorting your vision and hearing. Opoid analgesics have a painkilling effect.

Check your list. Can you categorise each drug by one of the four terms above?

A drug is defined as 'a medicinal substance, but also as a narcotic, hallucinogen, or stimulant, especially one causing addiction' (Oxford Reference Dictionary).

Does your list cover everything that would fit that definition?

When asked to list drugs, people often list illegal drugs – heroin, cocaine, marijuana and so on. They tend to forget those legal ones we meet on a daily basis – alcohol and tobacco. You'll find out later that these legal ones actually cause the most deaths, crime and violence of any drugs in our society.

Why do you think that may be?

For this Unit, you have to be aware of the range of drugs used legally and illegally by society, and the effect they have on their users, as well as on society generally. You have to be aware of trends to legalise, or not to legalise, certain drugs. You have to be able to put this knowledge into a religious perspective – how do religious traditions feel about the use of drugs recreationally and socially, or to enhance performance for example. What is the attitude of religious traditions to the effect these drugs have on the user? Is this the key to their attitude to the drug itself?

To get some idea of what the religious perspective is going to be, check back to pages 26–7. Bear that in mind as you find out about this Unit, and try to apply it all the way through. Keep answering the question – is this agreeing with, or going against, the ideas of Christianity (for example)?

Why Use Drugs?

Make a list of the reasons why people use drugs. You may be asked exactly that question in your examination. Are there different reasons for using different types of drugs? Try to give some examples of drugs taken for specific reasons.

Ask ten people why they first took a drug, and you'll probably get ten different answers. Ask twenty, you may get twenty. If your parents smoke or drink, ask them why they began, and why they continue – their reasons will be similar to the reasons why anyone takes any drug.

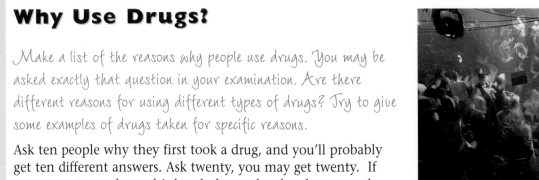

like the risk

it's fun

rebellion

easy to get them

curious

my friends do, so I do

bored

liked how it made me feel

escape

it's what people do when they go to X

makes me feel grown-up

So, someone whose life is tough, and has a lot of problems, may turn to drugs. Not everyone in that situation will, though – why not? It is a lot to do with how available the drugs are, as well as what they are actually like.

What about sportsmen and women? There have been a number of famous cases of people caught using drugs. Why do they take them? They obviously feel the potential gain outweighs the risk of getting caught.

We can classify drugs according to why they are used – as an experiment; as part of our social life (recreational drugs); to improve our performance; to make us feel better; to calm us down.

Can you fit any drug into any of these areas?

The Basics

① Name some drugs which are taken legally, and some which are taken illegally.

② Why do people begin to take drugs?

③ Why is it the case that not everyone in the same situation begins to take drugs?

④ Describe and explain two situations in which someone might begin to take drugs, showing why they make that decision.

⑤ As long as you don't encourage anyone else to take drugs, it should be your decision and your business, no-one else's. Do you agree? Give reasons and explain your answer.

SIX

Tobacco

Tobacco Facts

▶ About 13 million adults in the UK smoke tobacco – 29% of all males, and 25% of all females.

▶ In 1974, about 50% of the population smoked, now about 25% do.

▶ 80% of smokers started as teenagers.

▶ In the UK, about 450 children start smoking every day.

▶ About 25% of 15 year olds smoke, even though it is illegal to sell tobacco to them.

▶ 120,000 people die annually as a result of their habit – that's 330 per day.

▶ Smoking causes 30% of all cancer deaths.

▶ One in two smokers will die because of their habit.

▶ More than 17,000 children under 5 are admitted to hospital every year because of the effects of passive smoking.

▶ Over 4000 different chemicals can get into your bloodstream from smoking cigarettes, including DDT, tar, nicotine, arsenic, phenol, ammonia, naphthalene and cadmium.

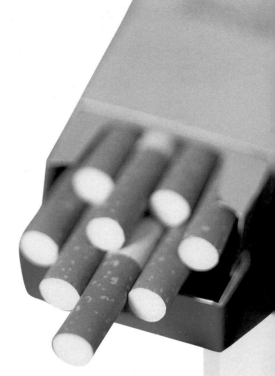

You have already looked at why people take drugs. Why should people give up? There are three major factors.

Why do people smoke? Are the reasons different to those for harder drugs? Why is it more acceptable to smoke?

Cost – if you smoke, work out how many a day. How many packs is that in a week? Multiply by 52 for the weeks in the year. Multiply by £4, for an average pack price. That is one year's cost to you. What else could you spend that money on?

Health – yours and those around you. Read on to find out the health cost to a smoker. Many people are ill, and die every day because of the smoking of others – passive smoking kills too.

The environment – smoking pollutes the environment, is an element of litter, and trees are cut down to make the cigarettes and their packets in the first place.

So, what does it do to you?

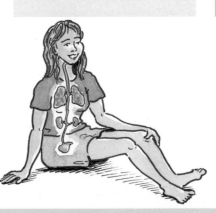

Short-term

● You smell (hair/clothes)
● Stains fingers and teeth
● Dries the skin (face)
● Causes wrinkles sooner
● Affects sports performance
● Bad breath

Long-term

● Coronary heart disease
● Emphysema
● Cancer of the mouth, throat, lung, bladder

Share and Share Alike!

It isn't only the smokers themselves who are affected by their smoking. Go back a page, what are the three factors for giving up smoking? Think about them in terms of their benefit to others.

A married man who smokes a packet a day costs his family how much? £4 a packet, £28 a week, £1456 a year. In just one year, that is enough for a family holiday (minus the spending money). Try multiplying it by years! Smokers affect the health of those around them, especially their families, who are forced to passively smoke which can make them ill. We all share the same environment – there aren't separate ones for smokers and non-smokers.

Passive Smoking

We inhale two types of other people's smoke – that from the cigarette tip, and that which they breath out. It does the same to everyone – it can irritate the eyes, nose and throat. It leads to headaches and nausea. It worsens existing, and causes new, respiratory illness. It increases breathing problems for asthmatics, and increases the number and severity of the attacks they have. For young people, it has a greater effect in all those ways, because children are still developing. It can also affect the normal growth of their lungs. For adults, it raises the chance of heart disease and cancer.

When pregnant women smoke, the baby smokes. Anything the mother takes in passes through the baby's system. Babies born to women who smoke are often underweight, often born prematurely, and are more likely to get respiratory illness, which is also more severe than normal.

Many establishments are becoming non-smoking places, because of the fact that one person smoking affects others (who don't want to). Restaurants have non-smoking areas, though this isn't the most effective – smoke doesn't take notice of no smoking signs! Companies have banned smoking from their premises. Many schools are no smoking zones – is yours?

Which places should definitely be non-smoking places?
Explain yourself in each case.
Do no smoking areas work?
Explain.

> ▶ *Organisation Profile*

ASH (Action on Smoking and Health) is an organisation which disagrees with smoking. Its aim is to preserve the health of the community by educating everyone about the realities of smoking. It tries to challenge the tobacco industry, which it feels is not honest about the effects of tobacco. Obviously, the future of tobacco companies relies on people being smokers. It is their business to increase numbers of smokers, not decrease them. Check out ASH, and the truth about tobacco at *www.ash.org.uk*.

Alcohol

Alcohol Facts

► Between 10,000 and 40,000 people die each year in the UK because of alcohol.

► Nearly half of all household fires are linked with someone who has been drinking.

► About 1,000 young people under 15 have hospital treatment for acute alcohol poisoning every year.

► In 1994, almost 60,000 people got criminal records for offences to do with drunkenness.

► Heavy drinkers/smokers are 150 times more likely to get throat/mouth cancer.

► Half of all adult head injury patients are drunk when admitted.

► In about half of all pedestrian fatalities in traffic accidents, the pedestrian involved had been drinking.

Alcohol has a better press than any other drug, yet probably causes the most problems of all.

Why do you think this is the case?

Most adults have tasted alcohol. Increasing numbers of young people have too. It is quite fashionable, and part of growing up, as far as some people are concerned. The law states that until the age of 18, it is illegal to buy alcohol, or for anyone to buy it for you. You can have a drink with a meal in a pub if you are 16 or 17, but that is the only exception. Even after the age of 18, you can't just drink what you want, where you want. More cities and towns are making it illegal to drink on the streets, for example, so you have to be at home, or somewhere licensed to serve alcohol.

Why do you think these regulations exist?

Alcohol affects people in different ways. In minutes, it has a depressant effect on your brain and central nervous system, so although it may make you relax and become happier, it is actually slowing down your system and your reflexes. This is why many accidents are caused by drinking – people just aren't as aware of the risks they take. Its effect depends on many things – your size and weight, how much you (normally) drink, what you drink, whether or not you have eaten – the list continues. Basically, it'll affect each of us slightly differently, at different times, and so we'll each recover differently at different times. Most of us are lucky to escape with a headache or an embarrassing story, but there is no guarantee.

What sorts of risks do we take when our judgement is impaired by alcohol?

In the long-term, alcohol can have a much more serious impact on us, and our families, and that is a major factor in why religious traditions don't agree with drinking alcohol.

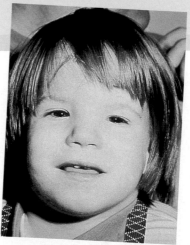

The Effects of Alcohol

You can have a great time when drinking, which is why many people do it. However, like most things it has to be done in moderation, to ensure there is not a heavy price to pay.

The Big Problems Caused by Alcohol

▶ The brain – one of the permanent effects of alcohol abuse is to reduce the amount of brain tissue, and increase the space taken up by ventricles in the brain. These help pump blood.

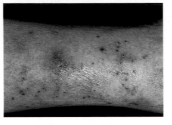

▶ The reproductive system – alcohol depresses nerve impulses, and an erection is a result of those. Some men can't perform because of the alcohol. One in three women who drink whilst pregnant have underweight, small babies, which often have reduced intelligence, and can have facial deformities.

▶ The heart – alcohol abuse leads to poor diet, which leads to vitamin deficiencies. One of these deficiencies can be a cause of heart failure.

▶ The skin – alcohol causes small blood vessels to widen, making you flushed in appearance. This becomes permanent in heavy drinkers.

▶ The liver – regular consumption of large quantities of alcohol kills liver cells. This is called cirrhosis, and is irreparable. A healthy liver is vital to good health, a damaged liver can kill.

▶ Weight – since alcohol contains sugar and carbohydrates, many heavy drinkers put on a lot of weight.

None of that tells you what effect heavy drinking has on someone's family. Many drinkers can be violent. If addicted to alcohol, their behaviour and illness affects their family in many ways. Alcohol makes you lose control – it can't be pleasant for someone to have to clean up their mum/dad on a regular basis, because they are always drunk. Alcohol also costs money, and loses people their jobs. Many of those who seek help for their addiction have already lost their families because of it.

▶ **Organisation Profile**

Alcohol Concern was set up in 1984, and was Charity of the Year 2000. It aims to reduce the incidence and costs of alcohol related harm, and to increase the range and quality of services available to people with alcohol related problems. It sees alcohol as a major issue, and wants to help with the solution. *www.alcoholconcern.org.uk*

The Basics

Answer separately for smoking, and for alcohol.

① Why do it?

② What effect can it have in the short-term?

③ What potential risks are faced with over-consumption?

④ What long-term effects can it have?

⑤ Outline the work of one organisation.

⑥ Use the information on page 26–7, to say how a religious believer in each of two traditions might view the overuse of either.

Think About It

It is important for you to be able to think around the topics. You will certainly have to answer an evaluative question, and must answer from several points of view if you hope to do well. You already know how to do this from Unit 2 Exam Tips. Most people have an opinion about drink and drugs, so let's take this opportunity to get some practice. You could do this page after you've found out more about drugs, if you don't feel like you know enough yet.

Complete this chart, saying how much you agree or disagree with each statement.

Compare your answers with a friend, and discuss your attitudes. Between you, try to come up with three reasons to agree with each, and three reasons to disagree. Then try to develop those reasons, so that each is fully explained. Being able to fully explain yourself is an AO2 skill, which you met in Unit 5.

	Strongly agree	Agree	No opinion	Disagree	Strongly disagree
Anyone caught experimenting with illegal drugs should be expelled from school/college.					
You need alcohol to make a social occasion go well.					
Smokers should have to pay their own health care bills.					
Cannabis should be legal.					
Alcoholics are a drain on the country financially and in social terms.					
Glue sniffing is harmless adolescent fun.					
People should take medication only when they desperately need it.					
Society has a duty to help heroin users give up heroin.					
People who work with young people have a duty to be positive role models when it comes to drugs.					
The drug you take depends on your cultural and social background.					
Children under 14 should not be allowed to drink caffeine-based drinks.					
The Government should make smoking and chewing tobacco products illegal.					
If people stopped smoking and drinking, the Government would lose millions.					
What you do in the privacy of your own home should be your business and no-one else's, as long as no-one is hurt.					

Let's Talk Drugs

Coke, charlie, snow, c, base   Rock, wash, stone   E, mitsu

This is only a quick look at drugs. Check out web sites such as
www.lifebytes.gov.uk and *www.release.org.uk* to find out more.
Local police forces, and Young Offenders Teams are usually
happy to come into school and give talks about drugs too.

Cocaine lifts the user, making them feel confident and wide-awake. It lasts about 30 minutes,
but can leave you craving more. Snorting can permanently damage the inside of the nose,
whilst heavy use can lead to heart problems, confusion and fits.
Becomes a habit. Class A.

Crack – makes users feel wide-awake and confident
for the ten-minute rush. Highly addictive, can
cause heart and lung problems. Class A.

Ecstasy – users feel wide-awake, and in tune
with surroundings, senses are heightened
greatly. Used by clubbers, because it lasts hours.
Has been linked to liver and kidney problems,
as well as deaths – due to dehydration. Class A.

LSD – trips last 8–12 hours, and the sensory
perception of the user is greatly affected. Can slow
down or speed up reflexes. Users hallucinate, and
these hallucinations can recur long after the trip is
over. Bad trips are terrifying. Class A.

Magic mushrooms – affect sensory perception. Can cause stomach pains, sickness and
diarrhoea. Class A when prepared.

Heroin – addictive. Users damage veins, put themselves at risk of infections and septicaemia.
Sharing needles can lead to infection with HIV, hepatitis etc. Class A.

Amphetamines – makes users
excited, confident and energetic.
Often leads to depression after it
wears off. Long-term use is linked to
mental health problems. Class B.

Cannabis – smoked, or used as food
ingredient. Relaxes users, makes them
talkative. Same risks as for smokers.
Can leave users feeling tired, with no
energy or motivation. Class B.

hash, puff, ganga, spliff, skunk, wacky backy   acid, tabs, trips, dots, microdots   mushies   smack, skag, brown, gear, H

Anabolic steroids – used by sportsmen and women to allow them to train longer and harder, and to recover more quickly after. Makes users more aggressive. Can increase production of hormones normally found in opposite sex within users, e.g. women growing facial hair, men growing breasts. Class C.

Tranquillisers – calms users down, relieves anxiety. Can be addictive and lead to memory loss, and giving up leads to panic attacks. Supplying is Class C offence.

Poppers – inhaled, these give a 2–5 minute 'head-rush'. Can give headaches, nausea, irritation to mouth and nose. Burns the skin if spilled. Prescription only.

Aerosols/glues – makes users feel like they are drunk, can make them hallucinate – affects the senses. Causes headaches and nausea, facial irritation. Long-term use causes damage to brain, liver, and kidneys. Users are at risk because senses are impaired. Illegal to sell to under 18s.

The law regarding illegal drugs comes under the Misuse of Drugs Act 1971. It lists three classes of drugs, and gives penalties for possession (having the drug for personal use), and supplying (having more than is needed for personal use, therefore intending to sell it).

- Class A drugs – 7 years imprisonment/fine for possession; life imprisonment/fine for supplying.

- Class B drugs – 5 years imprisonment/fine for possession; 14 years imprisonment/fine for supplying.

- Class C drugs – 2 years imprisonment/fine; 5 years imprisonment/fine for supplying.

▶ **Organisation Profile**

Release was set up in 1967, and is the world's longest running drugs charity. It tries to provide a range of services dedicated to meeting the health, welfare and legal needs of drug users and those who live/work with them. They provide information and legal support. Check out their work on *www.release.org.uk*.

The Risks ... Why We Stop, or Don't Start

There are lots of different types of risks to taking drugs – legal or illegal.

Try to come up with a list of risks, before you continue to read those on this page.

► Health risks – short and long-term, disabling and fatal. If you desperately need a fix, you aren't going to check someone's HIV status, are you?

► Financial problems – drugs cost money. If you are addicted, you need to take the drug, so the money has to be found. Hard drugs, such as heroin, lead people into hurting others to get the money they need. How do you cope when your mum steals your stuff to pay for her habit?

► Uncertainty – you never know exactly what you are taking, as drugs are rarely pure. The side effects could include death. Did you really intend to pay for cement powder and cocaine?

► Criminal risks – getting a record can get you the sack, or restrict the jobs you can do. It can also be a block to travelling. How many parents would complain if they knew a teacher had a record for drugs?

The Basics

① Name the four types of drugs, and how they work. Give examples of each.

② Why do people take illegal drugs?

③ In what ways do illegal drugs affect more than just the user?

④ Explain the law on drug misuse.

Why We Don't Take Drugs

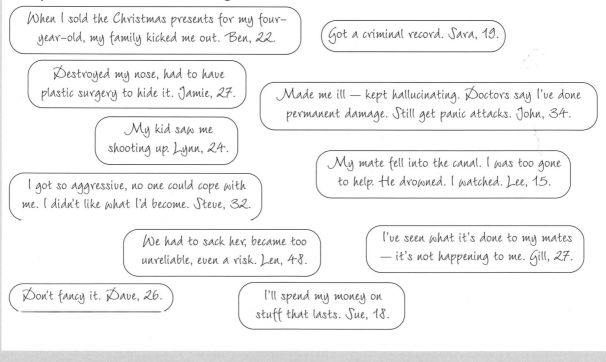

When I sold the Christmas presents for my four-year-old, my family kicked me out. Ben, 22.

Got a criminal record. Sara, 19.

Destroyed my nose, had to have plastic surgery to hide it. Jamie, 27.

Made me ill — kept hallucinating. Doctors say I've done permanent damage. Still get panic attacks. John, 34.

My kid saw me shooting up. Lynn, 24.

I got so aggressive, no one could cope with me. I didn't like what I'd become. Steve, 32.

My mate fell into the canal. I was too gone to help. He drowned. I watched. Lee, 15.

We had to sack her, became too unreliable, even a risk. Len, 48.

I've seen what it's done to my mates — it's not happening to me. Gill, 27.

Don't fancy it. Dave, 26.

I'll spend my money on stuff that lasts. Sue, 18.

Religious Traditions and Drugs

I follow the teachings of the Bible, and from the Pope, because **I am Roman Catholic**. There aren't any direct teachings about drug abuse in the Bible, so I rely on applying interpretations of the scripture to these issues. I know that God created me, and that I am a unique individual, it says so in Genesis. I also know that God regards me as very special – in Psalms it talks of how he knew me even in the womb. He let his own son die to save me from my wrongdoing. St Paul says that my body is a temple to God, so I should keep it sacred. Personally, I don't smoke, because of the health risks. You could say I am too special for me to do that to myself. I'd be disrespecting God, really, when I should be worshipping him. My religion doesn't say I can't though. I do drink alcohol, but within reason – the Church says it is immoral for a person to lose control like that. I agree, and it can damage your body – back to respecting God. The Pope has condemned drug abuse as the new slavery, because it takes away people's ability to choose for themselves. He says we must prevent drug abuse at all costs, and help victims to free themselves from addiction. Obviously, Catholics shouldn't do drugs, but we should not ignore drug users. Jesus said we can't enter the Kingdom of God if we don't help them, so it is in everybody's interests to do that.

I am a Muslim. For my religion, any form of drug taking, other than as medicine, is haram – forbidden. Prophet Muhammad called intoxicants the mother of all vices, and said that whoever drinks, Allah will not accept his prayers for forty days. Certainly to drink too much, or to abuse drugs is to harm yourself – this is forbidden by Qur'an and Hadith. When you have too much of something, you lose control of yourself and your mind. This would allow you to commit great wrongs, so is forbidden. Many Muslims smoke, but they shouldn't affect anyone else, and shouldn't encourage others to follow their ways. The wrong of intoxicants is so great, that it is forbidden for a Muslim to work in any stage of the process of making or distributing them. I have Muslim friends who would not go into a house where they knew there was alcohol. Prophet Muhammad ﷺ said a person is not a believer when he drinks – what if I drink, then die, how can I go to Paradise? It is important to help people who do these things though, so they can stop.

SIX

I am a Sikh. The Gurus forbade the drinking of alcohol, so it is quite clear to me on that issue. When I went through the Amrit ceremony to accept fully my obligations as a Sikh, I agreed to keep some rules throughout my life. One of these was that I should not consume any intoxicating substances. So, alcohol and drugs are definitely not allowed for Sikhs. These substances cloud the mind, so make it difficult to know what God wants us to do. They also damage your body, which is given by God. So to take these things is really an insult to God, because you aren't looking after this gift. Those who abuse alcohol and drugs also end up hurting their families in many ways, so again this is wrong.

Few Sikhs smoke, because it is unhealthy, and the Gurus promoted the idea of healthy living and healthy bodies. We just go against their teachings, as well as hurting ourselves, and wasting the money we should use for our families if we do these things.

Sikhism is a religion of service though, and following the example of the Gurus, we should help those in need. We could count any addicts as being in need. Many Sikhs choose to work in social care, and are involved in exactly this type of help.

The Basics

Use pages 26–7 also.

①
Choose two religious traditions. For each, explain their attitude to –
a. the body
b. who life belongs to

②
Use your answer to Q1, to explain their attitudes to –
a. smoking
b. alcohol
c. drug abuse

③
Explain how these believers might treat addicts.

④
Write a set of questions for your partner to answer about two of these religious attitudes.

I am a Methodist. We can drink or smoke, though some Methodists believe it is totally wrong to do either. You have to look after the body, which is gifted to us by God – it is sacred. As long as you consider the risks, and be careful, you can choose. God has given us many medicines naturally, so we have to accept it is right to use them, but in a medicinal sense. When it comes to dependency on a substance, that is not right. We become slaves to the substance, and turn away from God. We harm ourselves, and end up hurting others. As Christians, we want to be able to help those who have become dependent, and there is a long history of my church doing just that. We try to offer support and hospitality to these people and their families. We don't judge them – that is not helpful to anyone. What we want to do is help create a drug-free society.

SIX

Exam Tips

This is both an exam and revision tip really.

When you revise, you need to know an awful lot about each topic, but for that last minute revision it isn't helpful to have pages of notes. You need to have a shorthand form of the information. A good idea is to use a spidergram, where each leg of the spider triggers a whole lot of detail or associations in your head. This can also be used in the exam. When you are doing your exam, you will have time for thought, and can use that to get a skeleton structure for an answer. Don't take too much time over it – give yourself a few minutes of thought per question, and stick to the limit. Make sure you put the spidergram onto your exam paper, or hand in your note paper – if you had something on there that was worth credit, but hadn't written it in your answer, you should still get some credit for it. Never bin note paper from exams, unless the jottings have nothing to do with the subject!

Let's see a spidergram on Drugs, as a simple starter –

You can see you need to know what drugs there are, what the law says, why they are used, how they affect you and how we can help people. From those you could have other categories, either extra, or breaking those ones up further.

It doesn't take a great deal of work to turn that spidergram into an essay. Extend each element by splitting each one e.g. splitting *their effects* into the immediate effect, and the health effects. Add examples where you can, e.g. for *why people use them,* put in an imaginary scenario. Now write it out in essay form.

Try some others, first in quick form, then extended. Here are some suggestions, but you can do it for any topic and any GCSE really.

Topics
Religious attitudes to drug abuse
Why people take drugs – and why they shouldn't.
Alcohol
Smoking
The body and what we do to it

7 Religious Attitudes to Media and Technology

Introduction – Media Sources

In this modern world, we have access to many sources of information and entertainment, far too many for anyone to be able to use fully. This Unit looks at that range, and tries to consider the religious attitude to this explosion of information, and the increased accessibility there is to it. You can now learn about, see and experience through multimedia almost anything. The question is – do you want to? Or, more to the point, should you be allowed to?

Let's explore the myriad of media we can now access.

Newspapers – there are two types, which are broadsheet (e.g. The Times), and tabloid (e.g. The Sun). Newspapers are issued daily, weekly, or fortnightly. They can be free or paid for. They can discuss local, national or international issues, or all of them.

Magazines – hundreds of these! They can be generally for men, women, children; for particular interests and hobbies. Publication varies from weekly to quarterly. Cost can be very high. Magazines and newspapers are regulated by the Press Complaints Commission.

TV – terrestrial TV consists of BBC1, BBC2, ITV, C4 and Channel 5. It's available to anyone who will buy a licence for their TV set. An offshoot, which is really where TV came from, is radio. Although TV stations are national, they do have local variations within daily schedules.

Radio covers local and national stations. Much of broadcasting is paid for by advertising, which can put its own stresses and strains on what is seen/heard. They are regulated by the Broadcasting Standards Commission.

Satellite – a growing number of channels are available on cable and satellite, which increasingly cover wider and wider (and more and more personal) areas of life and the world. Payment of subscription fees grants viewing rights, as long as you have the equipment to receive the broadcasts. As the list of channels grows, so does the list of pay-per-view programmes and channels.

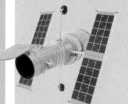

Cinema – films are produced across the world for viewing first at the cinema. In the UK, the British Board of Film Classification gives each film a licence, and a category. This category determines who can watch the film at the cinema. Films can be split into mainstream and special interest. You'd expect to see all the latest Hollywood films at your local cinema, but would you see the latest arthouse film?

Music – jazz, rock, opera, classical, pop – the list goes on. There are many styles of music, and people like a few, some, or all of them. Since music is an art form, it is often used to express the ideas and ethos of the performer/writer.

Internet – the world wide web, normally accessed by computer via a telephone line. As recently as 1993, fewer than fifty sites existed, in 2002 there are over 400 million. You can find out anything – if you have enough time to do it. Sites are for organisations, governments, businesses, special interests, children, adults – the list is literally endless.

① For each genre, list as many examples as you can. For example, list all the newspapers you know of, or the films you've watched recently at the cinema.

② Try to spot categories or characteristics within each list you write. For example, magazines could be glossy, or plain.

③ Could you work out what sort of people read/use the different types within each list, based on how they are presented? For example, websites aimed at young people are different in style to those aimed at professional groups.

④ Have you ever seen or heard something on each of the types, which you felt was not appropriate? For example, images of something that shouldn't be on TV, or an advert, which was offensive. What makes you think it inappropriate?

⑤ Since all forms of media are guided or controlled by organisations (most are businesses), with their own ethos and agenda, do you think this makes their content biased? Or does it just affect style of presentation?

⑥ Do you think there should be censorship of what we see? Or should we censor for ourselves? Explain yourself.

⑦ Do you believe everything you see or read in the media? Why/why not? Give some examples. In other words, is it all real — or just versions of the truth, if that?

How Media Affects Us

Why do we use media? List the reasons.

Your list might have looked like this –

- Inform
- Educate
- Entertain

But, what else do media sources do for us?

They also manipulate us – think of the advert that makes you want to buy something, or the programme that shapes your attitude to something.

They affect our behaviour – think of the children who copy what they see on World Wrestling Foundation (WWF) programmes.

Can you give examples for each of those reasons. Try to give positive and negative examples. Check out media sources for a week, and keep a log of each.

Are there times when the media goes too far? Is it possible to learn what you didn't want to learn, or be informed about something you'd rather not have known? Can you give examples?

The Effect on Children

There are many studies, which are concerned with how much children are affected by what they view in the media. Young children re-enact the things they see, without realising the actual consequences in real life. There isn't any proof that violence on TV or in film, for example, causes people to commit violent crimes. It is thought to encourage people into violence who already have psychological conditions, though, and to make people generally more aggressive. It certainly contributes to making someone believe the world is a very violent place, that the violence they see is normal, and that violent offenders usually go unpunished. They become desensitised to violence, and more fearful of being attacked. All of this has been proven in studies.

Child killers were obsessed with horror film

So, should we try to decrease the amount of violence in the media? Who should decide what is or isn't too much? Should it make a difference depending on who is watching?

Heist plan based on TV drama story

What about bad language? many say there is too much on TV. Even though a family might not use such language, their children hear it on TV and radio. Should there be controls on this?

And then there is sex – the amount and explicitness increases as you get later into the evening. Is it too much? Does this damage children, or does it educate them? Think about how it is portrayed, and therefore what message people get. If there are no appropriate consequences for inappropriate actions, children especially can get a skewed vision of the place of sex in a relationship.

Radio 1 apologises for Ali G's expletives in Breakfast Show

seven

Accessing the Media

Imagine you had control over media sources. Would you let channels show exactly what they want, or would you place restrictions on their scheduling? In this exercise, you have to decide which form of media you would use to showcase the programmes illustrated – TV, satellite or Internet. You have to decide the scheduling – at which times would you air the programmes? You have to justify each of your decisions – this exam likes you to be able to justify yourself, so you are going to get some practice here.

First, you have to come up with a set of rules about what can be shown by each media form. You must decide what you won't allow on particular forms, or at all. You need to include watershed rules (the watershed is the time before which certain images, usually violence and/or sex, and bad language, may not be shown).

Remember –

- most families have TVs;

- satellite is owned by over 60% of homes in the UK now, but can be used to show pay-per-view (no mistakes over seeing such programmes because you pay precisely to do that);

- the Internet is available in almost half of UK homes, and it can provide an interactive service, e.g. contributing questions for livecasts (a live broadcast).

Would you have liked to put any programme on the most widely available channel, but felt unable to? What were the pressures against this? Or for putting something in a particular place? The cost to the media of certain programmes decides how they are shown. Their popularity also affects that. The biggest control is censorship, which we look at next.

A steamy story of sex, love and broken promises

The top of the table clash which will decide the title

See Robbie Williams live and exclusive

A must for Simpsons fans everywhere!

STE CHALK. I WILL NOT WASTE CHAL
STE CHALK. I WILL NOT WASTE CHAL
STE CHA NOT WASTE CHAL
STE CHAL WASTE CHAL
STE CHALK. WASTE CHAL
WASTE CHAI
NOT WASTE CHAI

News on the Hour, as it breaks

#1 RENTON

Train spotting

#2 #3 #4 #5

Award-winning film. Some scenes may disturb viewers

Loud and clear, but don't let your gran watch!

The Friday sermon from Cheetham Hill Mosque

Censorship in the Media

Do you think censorship should totally be left to individuals?

Most people think there should be restrictions on what TV shows, that newspapers should be regulated, and that films should be rated, with those ratings used to control who sees them.

The Press Complaints Commission

This independent body deals with complaints from the public about newspapers and magazines. It uses a Code of Conduct, set up by the editors of British publications in 1999, to decide whether an article has gone too far. The Code tries to give special protection to vulnerable members of society, such as children, hospital patients and those at risk of discrimination.

Why does each need special protection?

The Code covers many areas, including accuracy, privacy, harassment, children, use of listening devices, misrepresentation, protection of confidential sources, and so on.

Why do you think regulation is important in each of these areas?

In 2000, there were 2225 complaints, of which over 60% related to the accuracy of an article, whilst 12% were to do with intrusion of privacy. You can find out more from their official website at *www.pcc.org.uk*

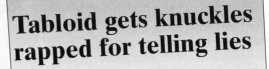

Tabloid gets knuckles rapped for telling lies

Broadcasting Standards Commission

The BSC is the statutory body for both standards and fairness in broadcasting. It covers TV, radio, terrestrial and satellite broadcasting.

BBC criticised for bad language

The Broadcasting Act 1996 set out three roles. Firstly, to produce codes of conduct relating to standards and fairness. Secondly, to consider and adjudicate on complaints. Thirdly, to monitor, research and report on standards and fairness in broadcasting.

If anyone is unhappy about a programme, they can complain on the grounds of its portrayal of sex, violence or other issues of taste and decency (e.g. bad language). The BSC then considers the complaint, taking into account the time it was shown, maker's intent etc.

Why might people complain in each of these cases?

Find out about the BSC, including some of its rulings from the website *www.bsc.org.uk*

seven

The British Board of Film Classification

The BBFC is responsible for film, video and DVD ratings in the UK. Whenever a new film is put out for release, the Board has to view and classify it under one of the seven classifications available. This classification determines who can/can't watch it. Some are not given a classification, making them illegal. You'll recognise the ratings symbols. It is easy for cinemas to regulate their customers, but not so easy regulating who watches videos. One way the BBFC has fought against this is by making films cut more scenes from videos, or by giving higher ratings than were given to the cinema version.

Do you think this is effective?

There are a number of laws which the BBFC works within – The Video Recordings Act 1984 highlights specific images as being potentially harmful, especially to young people. This leads to cuts in films, or higher ratings, and images include criminal behaviour, use of illegal drugs, violent or horrific behaviour/incidents, and human sexual activity. Other laws make it illegal to show scenes which have been organised/directed to involve cruelty to animals; illegal to show indecent photographs of children (under 16); illegal to show obscene work, which means that when taken as a whole, it can be thought to have a tendency to deprave and corrupt a significant proportion of those likely to see it.

Why do you think these sorts of scenes are banned?

You can find out about this in more detail, and about recent classifications, as well as explanations of decisions on classifications by visiting the website *www.bbfc.org.uk*

The Basics

① Explain the following words, and give examples to show you understand the meaning of each – TV, Internet, Satellite, terrestrial channel, censorship, watershed, regulation.

② How does the media impact on us?

③ Why do people have concerns about the effect of TV on people, especially children? Give examples to support what you say.

④ Describe the work of the PCC, the BSC and the BBFC. In each case, explain why it is important.

⑤ *Censorship is an invasion of people's right to choose. It should itself be banned.* Do you agree? Give reasons and explain your answer showing you have thought about more than one point of view.

Beyond Decency?

What classification would you give the following films? Could they be shown on TV – if so, when?

1 A film about a gay priest.
2 A film about the hijacking of a plane by terrorists.
3 A film about a girl with a mental illness, who is put into an institution.
4 A sci-fi film about alien abduction and the take-over of earth by monsters.
5 A film about a brutal serial killer.
6 A film about a child growing up in the Second World War.
7 A film about two people who meet and fall in love, but they are already each married to someone else.
8 A cartoon film about a gang of children and their adventures.

Was it difficult to give a classification? Why? What things would affect the classification given for each?

Religious Broadcasting

Ever switched on the TV on a Sunday only to find a programme about Christianity, or – worse still – a church service?! It is amazing how people groan when they inadvertently find such programming – as if it is on all the time. However, if you watch TV regularly, you'll find that there is a lot of religious stuff, you just have to be aware of it.

Were you one of those watching Dot Cotton agonise over a euthanasia issue in Eastenders? What about the ethical dilemmas met in programmes such as The Vice, where a police officer seems lenient towards prostitutes (who are themselves breaking the law)?

10.0 Monty Python's Life Of Brian (1979) (T) An ordinary man in Roman-occupied Palestine is mistaken for the Messiah and becomes a reluctant figure of worship. Controversial biblical comedy, starring Graham Chapman, John Cleese, Eric Idle, Terry Jones, Michael Palin and Terry Gilliam, with cameos by Spike Milligan and producer George Harrison. 46048

Those ethical dilemmas are often tinged with religious concerns and attitudes. In some programmes, central characters are religious. Religion is everywhere.

What Forms Does Religious Broadcasting Take?

Check out this week's programme listings for TV and satellite. Make a list of all the programmes you see which have some religious link. Try to categorise those links. The major forms are – *information*, for example a documentary about the Hajj; *evangelical*, for example the church services on Life (satellite); *character-based*, for example any vicar in a soap; *dilemma-based*, for example a debate to save a life in Casualty, or to allow death. There may also be school programmes, which inform and educate.

CHOICE 7.30 The Hidden Jihad (T) Imran Khan explores what it means to be a young Muslim in Britain. 999

Try another set of categories – check the listings again, and work out how often you see each religious tradition.

Is there a fair balance between all the major faiths? The UK is a multi-cultural society, can we see that from the listings?

In another way, are the programmes focused in one part of the week, or are they spread across the week? Each religious tradition has a special day, but is that obvious from the listings? How about the timing?

After all that, do you still think there is too much religion on TV?!

11.05 Son Of God (T) Developments in archaeology and history enable Jeremy Bowen to trace the life of Jesus with greater accuracy than before. (rpt) 414512

The Basics

① What ways do we meet religion in the media? Give examples of each.

② Explain whether you feel the broadcasting of religious programmes is fair in terms of all faiths.

③ *If there was more religious content in the media, we'd understand the world a lot better.* Do you agree? Give reasons and explain your answer.

④ *Religious programmes should be pay-per-view, or have their own channel, and not be forced on us when most people don't want them.* Do you agree? Give reasons and explain your answer.

Why are Religions Involved in the Media?

Religions can reach many people who might not otherwise be reached via the media. This can be very important in helping people understand a faith and its traditions and beliefs. In the modern world, it is important to have a better understanding of those around you – it helps generate harmony and peace. Prejudice often comes from ignorance, so the media can be used to combat this. Go onto the Internet, and type in a search for a named religious tradition. You'll find official websites, which can give you the actual view of that tradition, for example, the Church of England's website is *www.cofe.anglican.org*

Christianity and Islam are both missionary religions. There is a religious duty to spread their understanding of God and his laws, and to bring more people into the religion. The media is a good way to spread their message further, faster. There are increasing numbers of evangelical channels on satellite and radio, as well as the Internet.

QUEER AS FOLK
how much fun can three lads have together?

For many people who aren't able to attend their own place of worship as often as they would like to, the religious broadcasts bring it to them. Many famous people are interviewed, or give speeches on the radio, for example. By using the media, more people can share their message. This helps people to understand their faith in terms of the world they live in.

Censorship

All religious traditions have strong views on what is morally acceptable, and this leads them to support censorship in the media. In fact, it is fair to say that many religious traditions feel that censorship is too lenient. Society should protect vulnerable members, especially the young, and censorship should be a tool to do that. Many Christians would still feel that a number of programmes are inappropriate due to message or content. They are likely to corrupt the morals of the watcher. For example, the series *Queer as Folk* did not show gay men in a negative light, and so might be said to encourage homosexuality, not least because one of its central characters was a schoolboy. Most religious traditions condemn homosexual acts as sinful.

Some programmes are considered blasphemous, for example the film, *The Last Temptation of Christ*, which was boycotted and picketed by Christian groups when it first appeared in British cinemas. Blasphemy is the act of abusing the name of God – it breaks one of the Ten Commandments, a basic law of several faiths. The Internet has many anti-religious sites, which could be seen as a source of corruption.

The Basics
① Why do religious traditions use the media?
① Why do they condemn the media? Give examples.

seven

Exam Tips

The final examination asks one compulsory question from the Truth and Spirituality sections (Units One to Three of this book), plus a choice of three questions from up to six offered (Unit Four onwards). So you don't necessarily need to learn everything you have studied - good news. Be warned, though, unless you are brilliant at those three topics, learn a couple of extra ones to give yourself a choice. Your *favourites* might be really tough questions.

When you revise, break a topic up into small chunks – you could use the breakdown found in this book. *What are the elements of this Unit?*

First, you need to know some examples of media – learn the range, and some examples to give for each. Next, know the key words – blasphemy, watershed, censorship, evangelism, pornography. Next, make sure you know why groups demand censorship, and why there is a debate over how great that should be. Next, be able to say why religious programming appears, along with examples, which show the roles it fulfils. Finally, be able to argue any comment about the media being good as well as bad. *With a partner, try to make brief notes to cover all of that.*

Let's take a couple of those and practise. You actually know a lot more than you think you do, after all, how much - TV do you watch? - news do you check out? - time do you spend on the Internet? It's all going to help.

What about the debate over censorship? There are two extremes – no censorship, and total censorship in line with extreme religious views (where nothing against those religious beliefs would be allowed). Can you argue for each (human rights – protection of morality). Make lists of reasons for each, then give examples of each reason, and explain each reason more fully. Build up answers as you were shown in Unit 3.

Try these. Imagine each is worth four marks, but you need to give depth as well as range –

1 Why do people want religious broadcasting on terrestrial TV?

2 What reasons do parents give for monitoring and controlling the media sources their children have access to?

Now those *arguing* questions. They can be constructed as a dialogue between two people, which forces you to cover two sides. Again, build up your answer.

Try some, and for each give reasons, explain yourself, and present more than one point of view –

1 Parents have a duty to stop their children seeing unsuitable material. When their children do see this, only the parents can be blamed. Do you agree?

2 Films reflect real life, not the other way round. Do you agree?

8 Religious Attitudes to Crime and Punishment

Crime and Punishment Exercise

Look at this list of crimes. Now look at the list of punishments available under the English law. What punishments do you feel are fit for each crime? Justify your decision in each case. Explain the intention behind your choice each time. Do you prefer any of the non-UK punishments – why?

Life imprisonment

Fourteen years imprisonment

Seven years imprisonment

Five years imprisonment

Two years imprisonment

Six months imprisonment

Community service

Fine

Restraining order

Exclusion order

Compensation order

Curfew order

Suspended sentence (only enforced if criminal reoffends)

Probation order (required to meet Probation Officer weekly)

Attendance centre order

Disqualification from driving

Electronic tagging

1 A woman who killed her husband after years of being beaten up by him

2 A man who raped two women

3 A young woman who assaulted a nurse at a hospital whilst being treated for injuries sustained whilst drunk

4 A schoolgirl who stole items worth £65 from a clothes shop

5 A woman who defrauded £50,000 from her employers

6 A schoolboy who graffitied a bridge near the railway station

7 A man who mugged at least seven people

8 Someone who sold drugs in the schoolyard

9 A woman who drove her car for eight months without insurance or MOT

10 Someone who killed nine people

11 Someone who sexually abused a number of children

12 A man who set up a café for people to smoke cannabis on the premises

Non-UK punishments, which you might have preferred.

Capital punishment (execution)

Corporal punishment (physical punishment, e.g. whipping, loss of hand/foot)

Why Society Punishes People for Breaking Laws

On the last page, it was important for you to justify the decisions you made regarding choice of punishments. Society sets up rules, and we have to obey them, or face the consequences. The interesting thing is that people view things differently, so what one person strongly feels is wrong, another might feel it to be less so. That is why we have a judicial system, which sets tariffs for punishment, and doesn't allow judges to do what they feel. Some of your decisions would have been different if you knew more information. Try adding an extra detail, then letting your partner redo the exercise to see if they change what they originally decided.

Did you go for the non-UK punishments? Having those really lets you know what society feels about something.

You need to know why we punish crimes – the theory of punishment. There are five aims of punishment, and you probably came up with all of them in that opening exercise.

Protection – that we have to protect members of our society. So if someone is a danger to others in any way, they are removed from circulation to protect people. This could mean imprisoning a murderer, or enforcing a curfew on a burglar.

Retribution – getting someone back for what they have done. We repay their crime, by hurting them in some way. In Islamic societies, thieves lose their hand – society has made them pay for their crime. Taking away someone's liberty (imprisonment) is another way we pay people back, for example, giving a prison sentence to someone who defrauded money.

Deterrence – this is a punishment designed to make the offender not do it again, and to send a message to everyone else not to. In other words, to put you off from committing the crime. The US uses execution in this way – if you commit murder, you will be executed, so don't commit murder. On a smaller scale, driving under the influence of alcohol leads to a ban, a fine and maybe imprisonment, so most people don't.

Reformation – to try to change someone's ways, and improve them as a responsible citizen. A graffiti artist might have to do community service, which involves some other way of expressing themselves, e.g. working on gardens in local parks. Someone

who has been joy-riding might have to work in a physiotherapy unit which deals with road traffic accident victims. The punishment is designed to make offenders consider their behaviour and why it was wrong. From that they may modify their behaviour, because their values have changed.

Vindication – if we have laws, we have to punish those who break them, or there would be no point to the laws. You get a fine for not having a valid parking ticket, because the rule says you have to have one. The car park might be empty, and you are depriving no one of a space, but that's the rule.

Check back to your answers in the opening exercise. Did your motivations cover all of these? Look at each crime. How would you punish each, choosing from the five aims set out above? What you are doing is demonstrating that the motivation behind a punishment has a big impact on the style of punishment given, its severity and its length.

Why Do People Commit Crime?

Usually, there is a trigger, or immediate cause – greed, boredom, hatred, lust etc. For example, someone sees their partner in a passionate embrace with someone else, and assaults that person. However, there may be much deeper causes – the life you have, conflict with others, mental or emotional disturbance, social pressures. For example, a drug addict needs to pay for their drugs. This might lead to theft, prostitution, drug dealing – all criminal offences.

It is important to know why someone commits a crime, because the punishment needs to take account of that reason for it to be effective. For example, if a drug addict steals, then just locking them up is of no help, given the ease of drug acquisition in prisons. They need supportive therapies to escape the addiction or they will reoffend.

Look at the crimes on page 77, what might have been the causes, and how might the punishments be used effectively to combat those issues?

The Basics

① What are the causes of crime? Give some examples to demonstrate each.

② What are the five motivations or aims of punishment?

③ Give an example for each of a crime, and an appropriate punishment which would mirror the aim.

④ Which aim do you think is the most effective? Why?

⑤ Which aim is the most beneficial to society in the long term? Why?

⑥ *If all criminals were punished very severely, crimes would almost disappear.* Do you agree? Give reasons and explain your answer, showing you have thought about more than one point of view.

⑦ *In a civilised society, we should try to reform all criminals. Most are damaged people, damaged by others, and we should help them, not damage them further.* Do you agree? Give reasons and explain your answer, showing you have thought about more than one point of view.

Exploring Punishments

Imprisonment – Some Facts

Britain locks up more people as a percentage of total population than any other country in Europe. There were over 71,000 inmates by the beginning of 2002.

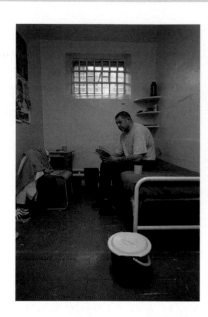

▶ Each prisoner costs the tax-payer about £35,000 per year.

▶ Over half of all prisoners reoffend within two years, this rises to two-thirds for young offenders.

▶ Twenty percent of all prisoners are on remand, which means they have lost their civil liberties until a trial has taken place. Of those, two-fifths will be found not guilty at trial, and will have to be recompensed for the time they served.

▶ Only a third of prisoners have committed serious offences (drugs, violence or sex-related).

▶ The majority of prisons are overcrowded.

▶ One prisoner commits suicide every five days, on average.

▶ Up to a third need psychiatric care, and would be better served by mental health care systems.

Do you think prisons are effective in any of the aims of punishment?

The Basics

①
Explain the terms – imprisonment; parole; community service.

②
Explain why organisations such as the Prison Reform Trust believe prisons need to be reformed.

③
For each of the three types of punishment mentioned on these pages, answer the following –
a. How does it tackle the cause(s) of the crimes, if at all?
b. Which aims of punishment does it reflect?
c. How effective do you think it will be?
Explain your answer.

④
Why do you think the UK seems to prefer to lock up offenders, rather than use other methods of punishment?

On Parole

This is also known as release on licence. It means that an offender is released from their prison sentence before they have completed the full time given them in their sentence. During the period of parole, which differs for different offenders, they have to live within the law. If they break the law, they will be returned to prison for the remainder of their original sentence.

Parole officers support them through this time, and try to take advantage of opportunities to help them re-integrate into society in a meaningful way. They have to meet regularly to discuss progress, and iron out any problems being met, perhaps by attending a probation centre. The parole order might require that they have to have specific treatment, e.g. for drug abuse. The parole officer can help them to access different services as part of this help. The idea is to help them avoid re-offending, as well as to help them integrate as responsible citizens who have the opportunity and ability to contribute positively. About 60% will reoffend within two years.

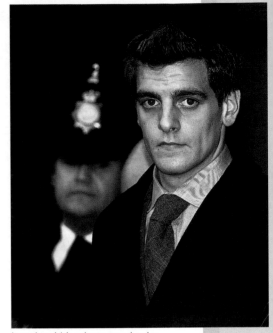

Jonathan Woodgate received a community service sentence for affray. He had to work on projects with children from deprived backgrounds.

Community Service

Instead of imprisonment, an increasing number of minor offenders are given community service punishments. The offender has to work within the community at a specific task for a number of hours (between 40 and 240). One high profile example of this was the Leeds United footballer, Jonathan Woodgate. He was sentenced to community service, having been found guilty of affray (using or threatening unlawful violence against someone to the extent that any reasonable person would feel afraid for their safety). In addition to his court sentence, his club made him work within their *Football in the Community* programme for the duration of his contract. This provides specialist football coaching to those children who would otherwise not receive it, often in deprived communities.

The aim of community service is that the offender gives something back to the community, to try to repair some of the damage they have done. It may be that they work directly in a field related to their offence, for example, a graffiti-artist being made to clean walls, or to paint schools. The punishment hopefully brings some sense of personal and community responsibility to the offender, which helps them to reform. This form of punishment is cheaper than the prison alternative, and studies show it to be more effective.

Find out about alternative types of punishment — electronic tagging, curfew, binding over. For each you find out about, match it up against the aims of punishment, and find out how effective it is.

eight

Religious Attitudes to Crime and Punishment

What we want to find out is which aim(s) the Christian attitude embodies, and therefore whether the judicial system in the UK follows Christian teaching.

The early prison system was brutal, and reforms were championed by Christians such as Elizabeth Fry. They saw a need for forgiveness and reform, not just retaliation.

Should Christians follow the laws of the land in which they live? Jesus said *Give to Caesar what is Caesar's, and to God what is God's,* which might suggest obedience to the laws of a land. Later, St Paul said that all authority is given by God. This means that God has given power to those setting laws, so Christians should obey. Where the two codes clash, obey God.

What about punishment? Much of Jesus' teaching is about forgiveness – he even said you should forgive someone *seventy times seven times*, in other words, as often as it takes. He did believe in justice, though, and said God would punish wrongdoers.

The Church of England supported the Government's moves in 1991 to reform sentencing, and increase the use of non-custodial sentences. They felt that this would better rehabilitate, and re-educate, offenders. They also point out that many crimes are a result of circumstances, for example, poverty. Major issues in society need to be resolved so that people don't turn to crime. In the long term, helping people see why their actions are wrong, and how they can function within the law, would mean fewer people re-offended, and society was improved. Those principles of forgiveness and reform were very important. The Church continues to support punishments that are not just retaliatory. It also supports prison reform, and justice in the judicial system. Many Anglican chaplains work in prisons, and within the system, giving spiritual support to those who want it (prisoners and prison workers). Their work stresses the unique importance of everyone and that God forgives anyone who is truly sorry for what they have done.

Read the following case studies. How might each religious group believe they should be punished? How does that punishment reflect religious morality?

James is thirty-three, and has a wife and two sons. Guilty of organising an armed robbery on a Post Office – his first offence. His family live in council accommodation.

Susan is twenty. Guilty of shop-lifting (twenty-seven counts considered). This is her fourth conviction. She is a drug addict. She has a three year old son, and her partner is also an addict.

Grace is fifty-six. Guilty of murder. She claimed she was defending herself against her partner who abused her. Has a history of medical treatment for depression.

The Quakers stress that everyone has something of God within them, even the worst offenders. This underpins their attitude to the penal system, so that they urge fair treatment of prisoners, as well as just punishments, which will help the offender to reform (restorative punishment).

'Our approach to crime and criminal justice is a reflection of our deeply held belief in the value of each human being as a unique, precious child of God...Each has the ability to grow and change, to make amends, to learn what is right.'

This clear stance comes from the earliest days of the Quaker movement, when Quakers were often treated as criminals because they did not follow the state religion. They learned that the prison experience could cause even more damage to offenders, or damage the innocent, changing both for the worse. They realised caring treatment, and programmes to re-educate or reform people are vital – the mark of a caring society.

The Quaker movement also speaks of the need to try to improve the conditions which generate crime, such as poverty. The Government has a great responsibility to tackle these issues, which have many implications.

What are they?

Elizabeth Fry was a Quaker — find out about her work in prisons.

At the heart of **Buddhism** is the Precept of not causing harm to other beings, with its corollary to help others. Buddhists are expected to try to become more compassionate beings, that is to show loving kindness. This comes through in the Noble Eightfold Path, which encourages right (positive) speech, actions and so on. Being a faith which believes in reincarnation, Buddhism states that all of our actions generate karma, which shapes our future lifetimes. Offenders create a punishment for the future by their actions, as well as the one the state imposes. It is important to help them see how they can make up for this, and not repeat the offence, which would lead to further bad karma. Hence, compassion is the key to dealing with offenders, but punishment should work towards reforming them. The Buddha himself reformed a bandit and murderer called Angulimala. He became a monk, working with the needy, and was eventually murdered by relatives of his previous victims. Even the worst of people can give to society, if given the right help.

Angulimala is now the name of a Buddhist society, which works in prisons, and with prisoners after release. Its work has led to the creation of a number of Buddha Groves in British prisons. These are places for peaceful thought. Angulimala sends practising Buddhists to visit prisons to encourage Buddhist prisoners in their faith, and to help others too.

The Islamic Attitude to Crime and Punishment

A thief, whether man or woman, shall have his hands cut off as a penalty.
(Qur'an 5 v38)

The woman and man guilty of adultery or fornication, flog each one of them.
(Qur'an 24 v 2)

We ordained for them; Life for life. (Qur'an 5 v48)

Most people, when asked about Islamic punishment believe it to be just like that – extreme. In fact, it might be the only thing they think they know about Islam.

Muslim law, *Shari'ah*, is both secular and religious, being based on the Qur'an, Hadith and Sunnah (holy book of Islam, and the teachings of Muhammad ﷺ and other leaders). An offender breaks God's law as well as man's law. Given the fact that Allah (God) is beyond everything, and should be submitted to, the breaking of a law has immense spiritual and temporal importance. Additionally, Shari'ah sets the community above the individual, and any crime against the community is classed as a crime against Allah.

There is an issue about intent though, which changes how any offender is dealt with. If the offence is committed when fighting in the name of Islam, or when fighting for one's country (e.g. a soldier killing), or out of need (e.g. stealing to feed a starving family), then the prescribed punishment should not be levied. Any person who is insane can not be convicted of a crime and punished, nor can any child who has not reached puberty.

There are three general categories of crime in Islam. Firstly, *jinayat* crimes, which are those involving killing or wounding. Secondly, *hadd*

offences, which all carry a fixed penalty set within Shari'ah law. Thirdly, *ta'azir* offences, which are meant to shame the offender. The first two aim to deter people from committing the crime in the first place, and to gain retribution for what has been done. The third is for reform.

Ta'azir punishments are decided at the discretion of the judge, both form and severity. This kind of punishment tries to take into account social pressure and change. Most Muslim law today is dealt with under ta'azir rules.

Hadd offences include murder (execution), highway robbery (execution), theft (loss of hand) and adultery/fornication (lashes). It might seem very harsh, but it is actually not common for a judge to award any of these punishments. There are very strict criteria which must be met before any hadd punishments can be carried out. For example, there have to be two mature and pious male witnesses. In the case of theft, the victim must be able to show they had taken sufficient security measures, or they can be deemed to have invited the theft.

Compensating the Victims

Islam's criminal justice system provides a place for compensation to be given to victims or their families. By accepting such, the offender can be given a lighter punishment, for example, life imprisonment as opposed to execution.

Before Islam, the Arabian tribes held grudges against each other, and they continued these disagreements through hurting or killing members of other tribes. If someone from one tribe killed a member of another tribe, the aggrieved tribe killed someone from the murdering tribe, which then did the same back, and so on. Grudges were passed down like inheritances at the death of tribal leaders. This is known as blood feud. Prophet Muhammad ﷺ changed this substantially, to make it possible to offer compensation for offences, which then made up part of the punishment. The compensation shows repentance for the initial act, and so should be accepted. For those who do accept compensation, they will also be rewarded by Allah for showing such mercy.

> We ordained for them: Life for life; eye for eye; ear for ear; tooth for tooth; and wounds equal for equal. But if any one remits the retaliation by way of charity it is an act of atonement for himself. (Qur'an 5 v48)

In recent years, perhaps the most internationally famous example of this was the murder of Yvonne Gilford, a nurse working in Saudi Arabia. The Saudi justice system found two British nurses – Lucille McLaughlan and Deborah Parry – guilty of her murder. At first, Yvonne's brother insisted on the death penalty. The judge at the trial seemed taken aback, because Gilford claimed to be a Christian. As far as the judge understood, Christians held forgiveness as a very important principle – this did not fit with demanding capital punishment. Eventually, Gilford accepted compensation, and the women were given prison sentences. The Islamic attitude is for equality in retaliation, which allows the death penalty in the case of murder, but makes clear provision for mercy and forgiveness also. Seeking retaliation is an understandable response, but mercy and forgiveness are obviously looked upon more highly.

Abdul Haq executed under insurrection laws

Pakistani lecturer executed for blasphemy

Zak'at social fund pays compensation fee for poor man who stole for his family

TEMPORARY INSANITY LEADS TO PRISON, NOT EXECUTION FOR WOMAN WHO KILLED CHILD

The Basics

① Choose two religious traditions and outline their attitude to punishment – why we should punish, and what the aims of the punishment should be. Use quotations where you can to support your account (use pages 26–7, as well as 82–5).

② Choose three crimes from page 77, for each of the two religious traditions you have just outlined. Try to explain how they would view those crimes, and what punishments they might give.

③ Do you think that more use of compensation awards for victims should be made? Explain how this helps reform an offender.

Capital Punishment

Capital punishment is the execution of an offender. It is a punishment reserved for the most extreme offences, usually murder, but can be used in other cases, for example, for blasphemy (showing contempt/disrespect for God), and for adultery by a married person.

Why So Extreme a Punishment?

The crimes are seen as so bad that no other punishment could be suitable. There is the idea of 'an eye for an eye' – exact revenge for a crime, seen as the *law of equality of retribution* in Islam. When you take a life, you deserve to lose your own. Because a murderer shows no respect for life, so we should mirror that in dealing with their life. Many holy books set certain punishments as execution.

The USA uses capital punishment. In 1977, the Senate lifted a moratorium on capital punishment, enabling states to choose whether or not to use it. Some re-adopted it as a punishment, via the electric chair, gas chamber or lethal injection. Since 1990, over 600 offenders have been executed, whilst many more still await execution on death row (they still have appeals pending). Amnesty International has said that the USA is savage, barbaric, cruel, prejudiced and uncivilised. This is because the USA has executed for offences committed whilst the offender was a child; those committed by mentally disturbed individuals; blacks sentenced by all-white juries after prosecutors had removed black jurors from the trials; where guilt was not definite; where defence had been inept; and foreign nationals whose right to help from their own governments had been denied. Current president, George W. Bush, was governor of the state with the worst execution record, Texas, where many unfair convictions led to execution.

Even within the USA, many dissenters exist – proven by the fact that not every state has the death penalty. 'The death penalty is a mirage that distracts society ... exacts a terrible price in dollars, lives and human decency ... it fuels (the flames of violence) while draining millions of dollars from more promising efforts to restore safety to our lives,' said a Manhattan District Attorney in 1996.

Use the following points to make up a dialogue discussing capital punishment.

To take a life is to say life is meaningless – that's how we should treat murderers.

Some crimes deserve the worst punishment.

A man takes a life, we take his – which is worse?

All life is sacred – including a criminal's.

The death penalty is barbaric.

These people are too dangerous to keep alive.

Life imprisonment is a waste of tax-payers money.

There is something worth saving in everyone.

What Aims are Met in Capital Punishment?

Retaliation, deterrence and vindication. Why these aims, and not others?

Religions generally disagree with the use of capital punishment. Even Islam and Judaism, which have capital punishment within their remit, prefer not to use it. Religious traditions all stress the sacredness of life. Christianity refuses to accept that any person is irredeemable – there is something of God in all of us. The Quakers point to restorative punishment, which capital punishment cannot be. 'A deep reverence for human life is worth more than a thousand executions in the prevention of murder; and is, in fact the great security for human life' (John Bright, first Quaker MP). In the UK, the death penalty was abolished in 1970, and the Church of England believes that its return would be totally wrong. Buddhists do not accept the use of capital punishment, since they believe it is wrong to harm another sentient being. The offender can do much to offset the bad karma they created by their original act, for example murder. They will suffer for this in a future life, but can make some repair in this. By executing them, we deny them this chance.

The Basics

① What is capital punishment?

② Why do some nations carry out capital punishment?

③ Use the notes from here plus pages 26–7, 82–5 to work out the attitude of two religious traditions to capital punishment.

④ *The death penalty shows we are just as bad as the offender.* Do you agree? Give reasons.

▶ Organisation Profile

Amnesty International was founded in 1961 by Peter Benenson, a British lawyer.

Today, it is the world's biggest human rights organisation, informing the world about human rights abuses, and campaigning for individuals, and political change. Amnesty sees no excuse for execution, seeing it as cruel, inhumane and degrading. In a recent report about the death penalty in the USA, it pointed out the degrading nature of that system, giving examples of prisoners being taken from intensive care to be executed, wired up for execution whilst awaiting last minute appeals, and a paraplegic being dragged to the electric chair. This isn't the sum of Amnesty's work, rather one part of it, because it is about human rights – any human should have those. You can find out about the work of Amnesty International, and more about the death penalty debate by checking out their website at *www.amnesty.org.uk*

Exam Tips

A starting point for your revision might be to make a list of the important words in each Unit. You can't answer any question if you don't know what key words mean. In the examination, an invigilator might be able to explain some words, but the examination rules will prevent them explaining the really important ones. We call this the technical language. There is a glossary in the back of this book, that could be your starting point.

What are the important words in this Unit? Try to make a list. Do you know what they all mean?

Your list should include

► Crime

► Punishment

► Deterrence

► Retribution

► Vindication

► Reform

► Protection

► Forgiveness

► Justice

► Capital Punishment

► Imprisonment

► Parole

► Community Service

There are probably more, but that is a benefit, not a hindrance.

Now you know the words.

1 What does each mean?

2 Can you think of an example to illustrate each?

3 Can you explain each, using different language to expand the total clarity of what you have said?

If you can do this, you are well on your way to knowing as much about the topic as you need.

The other element is knowing two religious attitudes. This is often what candidates find difficult, but it shouldn't be. Since it will be worth up to half the marks for each essay, it is important to learn it.

Choose a tradition. Pick out three points they make about the issue. Find a couple of quotations about it. Write them into a coherent paragraph.

Let's try capital punishment and Quakers.

Three points – something of God in everyone; restorative punishment; forgiveness.

Quote – *how many times shall I forgive my brother? Seventy times seven.*

So we get …

Quakers disagree with capital punishment. They say that there is something of God in everyone, even the worst offender. We disrespect God by taking their life if this is true. They believe in forgiveness, as Jesus forgave others, and taught in the Lord's Prayer. When he was asked how often someone should be forgiven he said seventy times seven, in other words as often as it takes. They also believe that punishment should be restorative because everyone is redeemable, going back to the idea of everyone having something of God in them.

Try that for another religious tradition. Then try it for punishment generally.

9 Religious Attitudes to Rich and Poor in Society

Introduction

What would make you happy? Could having money to burn be the solution to life's worries? Can you be poor and happy?

This Unit focuses on wealth, its accumulation, and its use. It considers how people become wealthy, how happy that wealth makes them, and how as religious people they might share that wealth to help others. On the flip side, it looks at why people find themselves in a state of poverty, and how that affects them.

We've all read the papers, and seen the latest lottery winners – and wanted to be them! We've also all walked past the homeless guy on the street, perhaps buying The Big Issue from him. How do you feel when you think about them? Who has put them into that position? Was it fate?

Why do people become rich or poor? Do you think any reasons are particularly positive or negative?

People's wealth may come from their family – they inherit wealth, for example, John Paul Getty Junior inherited billions from his father. It may come from the work they do, for example, Richard Branson built up his multi-million pound wealth through businesses, beginning with a record shop. It may come from gambling, for example, winning the lottery, or investing in stocks and shares (a more controlled gamble).

People may be born into poverty. They may lose all the money they have through bad business deals, for example, their business collapses and they go bankrupt, losing their home and everything. They may lose it through gambling, always chasing the big winner, which is always around the corner.

Managers of big businesses get paid huge amounts of money, known as **fat cat salaries**. At the same time, there are many people who are paid the **minimum wage**, and find it difficult to have enough money to provide for their family. There is massive inequality in our society. The religious traditions point to our relative wealth/poverty, and ask if we could better use our money. They don't see it as wrong to earn lots of money, but do stress that we should think how we can do good with the extra we have.

Is there a difference between being born into wealth/poverty, and suddenly acquiring wealth or becoming poor? Explain your answer.

You Just Won £3.2 Million!

Imagine winning £3.2 million. How good would that be? Actually, you couldn't, because it is illegal for those under sixteen to gamble. But let's imagine you were eighteen – and you've just won!

What sort of a difference would it make to the life of your family? If you had bought the ticket, would anyone else get a say in how it was spent? What would you do with the money?

Make a list of all the things you would buy with the money. Put the list into a priority order. With a partner, explain your choices and their priority.

Consider these questions:

▶ Who do you spend most on – you or others?

▶ What do you do with the bulk of your money – use it for yourself and your family, or something else?

▶ Do you continue to work, or look for work?

▶ Do you feel it is important to use that money to help anyone else?

▶ Have you got enough money to be happy?

Look at the people in these pictures. What sort of a difference would such a win make to their lives? How do you think they would spend it? Are there any who don't deserve it?

Read the following comments – do you agree or disagree with the sentiments of them?

> When you win a lot, everybody wants something off you, you suddenly get lots of new friends. It's very lonely being very rich.

> The lottery makes more people millionaires every week. Instead, I think that smaller sums of money should be spread out amongst more winners.

> There are people who spend more than they can afford to try to win the lottery, very few get lucky. The lottery encourages people to waste their cash.

> Gambling wins are mainly about luck, not hard work or expenditure, and always at the expense of the many more losers.

> It's a shock to win masses suddenly, people go silly with their cash, and waste it.

> Winning a lot means you can help people without ever touching your money, because of the interest. So you should.

The Other End of the Scale

Most people are not in the enviable position of having won a fortune. This Unit is more about people at the other end of the scale. You need to know about those who are homeless, and those living in poverty.

Homelessness

Did you know

- There are over 400,000 homeless people in England, including those who sleep rough, those in B & Bs, and those in squats.
- About 90% are male.
- Family conflict is the main immediate cause of homelessness amongst at least two thirds of homeless young people.
- A third of young homeless people have tried suicide.
- White women, and people from ethnic minorities make better use of social networks, so that the majority of homeless are white males.
- Mental health problems are four times as common amongst the homeless compared to society norms.
- One in two has been assaulted whilst homeless.

Living in Poverty

Did you know that some of the worst paid jobs in our society include shop work, hairdressing and security work? All paid around £4 an hour in 2001. That sort of wage is unlikely to cover the normal costs of weekly family life. The legal minimum wage is currently £4.10 an hour.

Did you know that in 1994, 3 million families relied on moneylenders, who charge between 100 and 500% interest? There are even more now. Those borrowers often can't get money anywhere else – and they can't repay what they borrow because of the interest.

Did you know that the Government has a Social Fund that people can borrow from, to repay at low rates? Unfortunately, the number requesting has gone up drastically, and the number failing to repay so getting blacklisted, has rocketed.

We live in a society where material goods are valued highly. You have to have all the new gadgets, or you are excluded. As people struggle to keep up, more and more get left behind, and become part of the growing numbers of those living in poverty. It has been said that poverty is a battle of invisibility, a lack of resources, exclusion, powerlessness... being blamed for society's problems. It is about a lot more than having no money.

▶ *Organisation Profile*

Crisis is the national charity for solitary homeless people.

Fighting for hope for homeless people

Crisis UK. Reg charity no. 1082947

It works year-round to help vulnerable and marginalised people get through the crisis of homelessness, fulfil their potential and transform their lives.

It develops innovative services which help homeless people rebuild their social and practical skills, join the world of work and reintegrate into society.

It enables homeless people to overcome acute problems such as addictions and mental health problems.

Whose Job is it to Help People?

Bill – I'm a manager of a big city company. I earn over £150,000 a year, plus bonuses. I have been criticised for my wage – fat cats, the papers dubbed my  colleagues and me, as if we didn't deserve the money. We all work tremendously hard for the money we get. We shoulder huge responsibility, managing business interests, which run into millions. On our decisions, the jobs of thousands depend. We work long hours too, even socialising is often in the name of our work.

I do contribute to helping those less well off than myself, you know, I give to several charities. I think we have to help such people help themselves.

Dave – I work on an assembly line, now I've left the army. I had a mate in the forces who became homeless – it's common amongst ex-servicemen, you know. Anyway, I decided I wanted to be involved and helping, so I do a night a week as a volunteer at the hostel in town. You see all sorts there, and loads have illnesses or drink/drug problems. Some of them could never fit back into living in their own place – been on the streets too long. Anyway, I can't afford to give a load of money, so I give my time. In some ways, I think it is more effective.

Ellen and John – We won some money on the lottery. A few of us in a syndicate won, actually, and got about half a million each. Anyway, it is more than we'll ever need, and we've no children. We gave a bit of it away to set up a local co-operative bank. We lent it to them to get started really, so we will get it back, but we won't take any interest on it. The co-operative lends people money at very low rates of interest. Lots of loan sharks round here, who charged people ten times the money they'd borrowed in the first place. We've been in that state, so wanted to help make a change. It's wrong that folk can't get stuff for their kids, or to be able to live properly.

Hannah – I run my own business. I take on two new workers every year, and train them up so that they can go on to get jobs in the business. I can't pay loads, but I choose people who I know need a chance. Maybe they didn't do well at school, but there's something about them. Maybe they have had problems at home, but I think I can trust them. Someone to believe in them, that's what they need.

nine

Steph – I'm a vicar, and I believe that I have to help the poor. It is part of my duty as a Christian. I got a job in a church in the inner city specifically to be able to do that. Jesus helped those in need, I try to walk in his footsteps. I went on parades last year to try to get the Government to change things – part of the Debt on the Doorstep campaign run by Church Action on Poverty (of which I am a member). Whatever I can do, I will – my job gives me lots of opportunities to try to influence people who can give something. I also do lots of counselling and ministering, so I hope I can help them spiritually.

Jane – I work for a charity, which tries to have an impact on poverty in Manchester. The people I work with often got into poverty after a bad run of luck, and once there they can't get out. They might have had a low paid job, which they lost – maybe through redundancy, but without a big cheque. Then they don't adjust to their new lower income quickly enough, and they get into debt. Ever borrowed money from a lender? Bad news, you pay back five times as much if you're lucky, usually it's a lot more. You've got to borrow more to pay the first lot off. We try to help people get out of that cycle, and into a state where they can begin to cope again, and to function again. You have to remember being in that state takes away everything – dignity, power, value. You become invisible, and feel like you just don't count any more – no one cares.

Read these accounts. What ways of helping are given here? Why does each person help? Can you add any other reasons to the list of why people feel they should help those in need?

The Basics

① Define *wealth* and *poverty*.

② Why are people rich?

③ Why are people poor?

④ Why are there always homeless people, despite what Governments and charities do?

⑤ In what ways is it true that people who live in poverty are powerless and invisible?

⑥ *People should get tough with themselves, then they'd get out of the problems they made for themselves.* Do you agree?

⑦ *Poor areas have the worst schools, highest crime rates and worst facilities. No wonder they stay poor. The Government needs to sort the areas out, if it wants to sort out poverty.* Do you agree? Give reasons and explain your answer.

nine

The Christian Attitude to Helping Others

The syllabus gives quotations for each of the topics, which candidates are expected to be aware of, and to use in their examination. On this double page, you can see all of the Biblical quotations for this topic. Read them, and then complete the task.

The Parable of the Sheep and Goats

This story, told by Jesus, is found in the Gospel of Matthew. Jesus had been teaching his disciples, and this formed part of it. He spoke about the end of time, and the coming of the Kingdom of God. He said that all people will be gathered

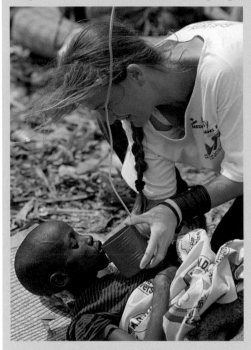

together, face to face with the Son of God. They will then be judged and despatched to heaven or hell. Those on the right hand side are called the sheep, they helped others, and by helping others, helped the Son of God. They will go to heaven. Those on the left are called the goats. They didn't help others willingly, and so will go to hell. The motto of the story seems to be that we should look for opportunities to help others, and we will be rewarded. When we help someone, we are helping God.

Matthew 6 v1–4
Some people, when they help others, make a big show of it. They take all the credit that they can. Jesus said that this was wrong. Any help given should be seen only by God, because then it is done out of compassion, not for plaudits.

Luke 3 v10–14
Jesus teaches that if someone has more than they actually need, they should share the excess with those who have too little. He also says that people should not cheat others for money – they should take only what they are owed. He also says that people should not abuse their positions of power to extort money from others.

Luke 10 v27
Love your neighbour as yourself.

Matthew 6 v19–21
Here Jesus pointed out that you can't take material goods to heaven with you. He said it is wrong to hoard wealth, so that robbers can steal it. Use it for good, because how you use it will be important at the Day of Judgement.

Matthew 6 v24
No one can serve two masters – money becomes a master. Serve God.

James 2 v14–19
This talks about someone's faith being useless to them, if they haven't carried out any good acts. In other words, your faith is about how you act, not just how you think. If someone needs something, as a Christian you have to help them.

① What message about personal use of wealth is found within each of the Biblical passages?

② What message about helping others is found within each of the Biblical passages? (who to help, and how to help?)

③ Explain why Christians should help others, using these Biblical passages to provide supporting evidence.

④ Should Christians be wealthy?

⑤ A church which is in solidarity with the poor can never be a rich church. Do you agree? Give reasons and explain your answer.

Acts 2 v45
This describes how the early Christian community, which was both poor and persecuted, was told to pool everything they had. The total was then redistributed fairly.

Mark 10 v17–22
Jesus is asked how it is possible to gain eternal life – in other words, how do you get to heaven? Jesus answers that it is necessary to keep all the commandments. When told by the enquirer that he had done that all his life, Jesus told him to go and give away his wealth to the poor. The man could not.

Matthew 19 v24
It is easier for a rich man to go through the eye of a needle, than to enter Heaven.

1 Timothy 6 v9–10
The love of money is the root of all evils. This love stops people from following their faith.

You actually have the basis for an answer to almost any question about how and why Christians help others in need, and about the use of personal wealth. This Unit is as much about the personal decisions we make to help or not help others, as it is about organisations, which help. You need to build up your knowledge on that.

nine

How Christians Demonstrate this Attitude

CHURCH ACTION ON POVERTY

The Church of England Stance

How we use our wealth is very important. The teachings of Jesus tell us to help others, and suggest we should do that in whatever way is available to us. Wealthy people can use their wealth to help others, and as Christians should do. People who are not wealthy should not waste their money either. In this respect, gambling is a waste of money – many families who have little money to spend – gamble, for example, on the National Lottery. They can't afford this, and the lottery offers a dream of wealth to them. The Synod of the Church of England is especially worried about the growth of personal debt. It asks its members to try to educate people about the danger of debt, and to teach money management.

In 1985 and 1990, the Church of England published two reports – *Faith in the City/Country*. These condemned the conditions that people found themselves forced to live in, and called upon the Government to work for change. It criticised the Government's use of the Social Fund, claiming that it just got people into further debt. Radical change is needed. It still says this. The Church itself has social funds which communities can tap into through their church, and is trying to contribute to the regeneration of communities in cities.

> ### ▶ Organisation Profile
>
> Church Action on Poverty (CAP) is a national ecumenical Christian justice charity. It is committed to tackling poverty in the UK. It works in partnership with local churches, and the people/communities in need. CAP believes that the message of Jesus was to help others, and that that message calls them to 'stand alongside those for whom poverty is a daily living experience'. It believes there is a very political side to poverty, because people who live in poverty become excluded from society in many ways. This means they don't use their right to vote, and have no say in the political process. They haven't the money to be involved in many things, and so disappear socially. CAP has run many campaigns to try to make change happen. An example is their campaign for a living wage, that is, a wage that it is possible to exist on in a meaningful way. The legal minimum wage is not enough to allow someone to have a healthy diet or have suitable clothes in winter. People on minimum wage make use of loans, and get into debt. CAP estimates a living wage would be between £5.80 and £6.30 an hour – compared to the £4.10 legal minimum, when the campaign was happening (2002).
> Find out more at *www.church-poverty.org.uk*

The Salvation Army

The Salvation Army was set up by William Booth in the 19th century. Its mission statement is to proclaim the Gospel, persuade people of all ages to become practising Christians, and to be involved in a programme of practical concern for the needs of humanity. Jesus' message was one of love, God is love, and the Army tries to mirror this in its work. Jesus' message was also that faith without good deeds is useless, so they combine both. The ministry element of the statement means that the Army comes into contact with many needy people, and so it is ideally placed to be able to offer help.

Its first shelter to feed the hungry and provide beds for the homeless was set up in 1887 by Booth's son, at Booth's command. Today there is a nation-wide network of homes, hostels and other centres. The Army also runs soup kitchens, and has a team of outreach workers in London who specifically work on getting the homeless back into permanent accommodation, through support.

The Army believes that gambling is wrong, because winning comes at the expense of others, and happens by chance. Since gambling is addictive, the families of gamblers suffer greatly from deprivation. Many families gamble to try to get a better life, but few actually win, so gambling just makes their problem worse.

Find out about the Salvation Army at *www.salvationarmy.org.uk*

The Basics

①
What is the Christian attitude to helping those in need around us? Use quotations to support your answer.

②
Describe the attitude of two Christian groups to the issue of the homeless.

③
Describe the work of one organisation working to alleviate problems faced by the homeless and the poor.

▶ Organisation Profile

The Catholic Housing Aid Society (CHAS)

This society believes in the equality and dignity of all humans, so that everyone has the right to adequate shelter. It is committed to social justice, which means that everyone within a community has equal chance and equal rights. Where poverty exists, it must be fought. CHAS works in a direct way to provide advice and assistance to those who are, or are in danger of being, homeless. It also educates by working with churches to raise awareness of homelessness and poverty, and to try to have an influence on housing policy at local and national levels. Find out more at *www.chasnational.org.uk*

The Jewish Attitude to Using Wealth

Charity is considered very highly in Judaism, in fact, in the Talmud, it says that charity is higher than the commandments. *Tsedakah* is charity. Judaism believes that a poor man's right to food, clothing and shelter is a legal claim which must be honoured by those more fortunate. It is an act of justice in the first place.

> Deuteronomy 15 v11 *You shall open your hand to your brother, to your poor and needy in your land.*

It isn't difficult to see that Jews must help the needy. Maimonides, one of the Jewish writers of the Talmud, said that anyone who can afford it, should give to the poor, and should do so cheerfully, compassionately and comfortingly. The worst kind of giving is that done grudgingly. He said that the highest form of giving was to help someone become self-sufficient, for example, giving them a job.

It is common for Jews to lend money to those in need. This takes away the stigma of being in need, because there is the understanding that it should be returned (though that is not necessary). It is forbidden in the Torah for one Jew to charge interest on a loan to another Jew, though they could charge interest to non-Jews. This is because non-Jews do not give free loans.

Use these quotations from the Tenakh (Christian Old Testament) to get a fuller idea of the teachings behind the Jewish attitude to money and its use in regard to the poor – Amos 8 v4-6; Psalm 146 v5–7; Deuteronomy 15 v7–8.

Find out about *World Jewish Relief* by going onto their website at *www.tolife.info*

The Ethics of Wealth

Look at these pairs of statements. Can you pick out arguments for and against from them? Add to your list to give a full consideration of the issue.

Issue – Wages

> I work really hard for my £4.10 an hour. I have a family — wife and kids. I do security work, so I work twelve or fourteen hour shifts most nights. In a way it is good that I work evenings/nights, because we couldn't afford to go out on what I earn. We get by, but it is really tough, and I'm happy to go without for the kids to have more or less what they need.

> I work really hard for my £250,000 a year plus. I am in important meetings most days, and have to deal with bosses of big companies across the world. I am responsible for a workforce of several thousand, and our product goes to twenty countries worldwide. People might say 'fat cat', but I work for it all. I am able to invest, so I can retire at fifty.

Issue – the Lottery

> I think it's brilliant. I spend about a tenner a week on the draws, and try my luck with some scratch cards, too. I regularly pick up a tenner — about once a month. I once won four thousand on the draw. I figure that one day I'll make it big. You've got to speculate to accumulate, though, so I keep trying. A big win would get it all back, and then the kids can have whatever they want. I tell them to just wait.

> The Lottery puts a lot of money into charitable causes. It isn't just lining someone's pocket. So I think it is a good idea. It is like a way of getting people to contribute, when they wouldn't if asked. I suppose more of it could go to charity though, and quicker. Maybe more people could win smaller prizes, instead of one mega prize. Have five smaller ones — you'd still win a fortune.

Issue – Taxation for Equality

> I pay enough taxes, and if I want to give to charity I do. It shouldn't be forced on me through tax. My money, my choice. I also want to be able to choose where my money goes — I don't think everybody deserves it.

> I think it'd be a good idea, because it would mean everybody contributed. At the moment, it's just a few, and the state of Britain is everybody's problem. It could be me who ends up on the street — just a bad break. I think projects to help people help themselves should exist, and we should make sure they do.

Exam Tips

In the exam, you have to have a cool head really, and not panic. The most important skill is that of being able to answer the question that is set, rather than the one you either wanted to read, or the one that relates to what you have learnt, or the one you think it says. Read carefully.

There are some questions which are easily misread, or misanswered. Let's take a look. What is wrong in each answer?

1 **Why do some religious believers disagree with gambling? (4)**

They think it is like stealing, because the winners get their money from everyone else, and didn't work for it. The Lottery does a lot of good though, because they give that money to charity as well as to winners.

2 **How can religious believers help those in need? (3)**

They should help because they will get a reward in heaven from God. Their religions all tell them to help others, as if it is a religious duty even, for example, Jews can give tzedakah (charity) which is supposed to be really good.

3 **Explain the attitude of one religious tradition to the use of personal wealth. (4)**

Christians believe that you should help others with your wealth, maybe giving them spare food or clothes, for example. Most people have spare time, and they can help out in soup kitchens, or charity shops.

4 **Explain two reasons why people become poor. (4)**

People might lose their job. They might have a row with their parents and get kicked out.

1 This answer doesn't answer the question, it actually goes off the point. The question wants to know why believers disagree. The answer begins that way, but gets side-tracked into a discussion about the Lottery and its value.

2 The answer is *why* not *how*, so it isn't worth anything.

3 There is no explanation of attitude. These questions want you to talk about what the teachings are from a tradition about an issue – what does the Bible say, for example. If you get into a speech about the things they do, you won't answer the question. Your answer will be too vague.

4 The question asks for an *explanation*, but the answer just *states*, i.e. gives two reasons. Look at the available marks, it must need more than simple reasons to get the full quota.

Re-read those questions, then write perfect answers for each one. Keep the available marks in mind – use that to help judge length of response. Be specific, not vague, when talking about religious attitudes.

Appendix 1

Tables for Levels of Response

Evaluative Questions (AO3)

Level		
Level One	One mark	Simple justification — I agree because ....
Level Two	Two marks	Opinion supported by one elaborated reason, or two or more simple reasons (for same or different points of view) I agree because of .... and .... Also ....
Level Three	Three marks	Opinion supported by one well-developed reason or two elaborated reasons I agree because ...., which means ....
Level Four	Four marks	Two distinct points of view, each explained or supported; there has to be evidence of reasoned consideration, i.e. perhaps including examples and quotes as support. I agree because......, Others might disagree because.... (plus explanations).
Level Five	Five marks	A clearly and fully explained answer, which gives good balance and weighting to both sides of the argument. Will include quotations and examples to fully develop the points being made. In some ways I agree for these reasons..., for example..., but in other ways I disagree for these reasons ...., for example.

Appendix II

Revision Checklist

This breaks the Course down into its constituent Units. Each Unit
can be split into words to learn, or glossary, and the elements to
understand. Use this as a checklist to guide your revision.

UNIT	WORDS TO LEARN	ELEMENTS OF UNIT
Nature of Truth and Spirituality	Truth Spirituality Scientific Truth Historical Truth Moral Truth Spiritual Truth Experience Belief Trust Faith Evidence Proof Probability Certainty	What is truth? Types of truth. Importance of each type of truth. Strength of each type of truth. Why people have religious faith. Faith v Reason. The nature of spirituality —soul, awe, inspiration, God.
Claims to Truth	Holy books Religious teachings Conscience Revelation	Claims to truth by religious authorities in 2 religious traditions. Claims to truth by sacred writings in 2 religious traditions. Claims to truth by conscience in 2 religious traditions. Strengths and weaknesses of each
Some Ways of Expressing Spirituality in Society	Symbolism Piety Creativity Membership Responsibility Community	How do people express religious commitment in 2 religious traditions? How do people support voluntary organisations in 2 religious traditions? How do people enjoy membership of 2 religious traditions?
Religious Attitudes to Matters of Life	Sexual intercourse IVF AID/H Surrogacy Sanctity of life Human genetic engineering Embryology Cloning Transplant surgery Blood transfusion	Why people want children. Artificial methods of conception. Is genetic engineering morally acceptable? The debate about blood transfusions. The attitude of 2 religious traditions to artificial methods of conception. The attitudes of 2 religious traditions to medical science.

UNIT	WORDS TO LEARN	ELEMENTS OF UNIT
Religious Attitudes to Matters of Death	Nuclear family Extended family Hospice Life support machines Sanctity of life Quality of life Active euthanasia Passive euthanasia Voluntary euthanasia Involuntary euthanasia Suicide	What 2 religious traditions believe about life after death. The issue of who life belongs to. Why people commit suicide. The attitudes of 2 religious traditions to suicide. Arguments for/against euthanasia. The issue of playing God. The attitudes of 2 religious traditions to euthanasia. The Hospice movement. The attitudes of 2 religious traditions to the elderly and their care.
Religious Attitudes to Drug Abuse	Social drugs Recreational drugs Performance enhancing drugs Hard drugs Soft drugs	Different types of drugs and their effects. Legal classification of drugs. Why people take drugs. The arguments for/against drug abuse. The attitude of 2 religious traditions to drug abuse.
Religious Attitudes to Media and Technology	Blasphemy Internet World wide web Website Satellite broadcasting Terrestrial television Categorisation of films Censorship TV watershed Pornography Evangelism	Different types of media. Censorship in the media. The debate over how much control should exist and who should have it. How religion is portrayed in the media. The effects of media on the viewer. The attitude of 2 religious traditions to regulation of the media. Religious use of the media.
Religious Attitudes to Crime and Punishment	Protection Retribution Deterrence Reformation Vindication Imprisonment Parole Early release Capital punishment Community service	Types of crime. Why people commit crime. Types and aims of punishment. The effectiveness of different types of punishment. The attitude of 2 religious traditions to crime and punishment. The issue of capital punishment. The attitude of 2 religious traditions to capital punishment.
Religious Attitudes to Rich and Poor in Society	Inherited wealth Indolence Minimum wage 'Fat cat' salaries National Lottery	Why people become/are wealthy. Why people become/are poor. How people help those less fortunate. The attitude of 2 religious traditions to helping others. The debate about helping others, and who is responsible for that. The attitude of 2 religious traditions to the use of personal wealth.

Appendix III

Sample Paper

The only section you complete on this page

Surname					Other Names						
Centre Number						Candidate Number					
Candidate Signature											

Leave blank

General Certificate of Secondary Education
Summer 2003

RELIGIOUS STUDIES (SPECIFICATION B)   **3062/74**
Paper 4 Truth, Spirituality and Contemporary Issues

Dateline

But if you use up all t lined sheets in this booklet, ASK FOR MO

In addition to this paper you will require:
no additional materials.

For Examiner's Use	
Question	Mark
1	
2	
3	
4	
5	
6	
7	
Q WC	
TOTAL	
Examiner's Initials	

Truth and Spirituality question

Time allowed: 1 hour 45 minutes

Instructions

- Use blue or black ink or ball-point pen.
- Fill in the boxes at the top of this page.
- In Section A, you **must** answer **Question 1**.
- In Section B, you should answer **any 3** questions chosen from **Questions 2 to 7**.
- Write your answers to Question 1 in the spaces provided in this booklet.
- Write your answers to all other Questions on the continuation sheets at the end of this booklet.
- If you use any additional sheets, tie them loosely to the back of this booklet.
- No more than **two** religious traditions should be used in your answer to any one question.
- Do all rough work in this book or on the continuation sheets. Cross through any work you do not want marked.

Quality of written communication—worth three marks at the most

Information

- The maximum mark for this paper is 83.
- Mark allocations are shown in brackets.
- You will be awarded up to 3 marks for quality of written communication. You are required to:
  - present relevant information in a form that suits its purposes;
  - ensure that text is legible and that spelling, punctuation and grammar are accurate, so that meaning is clear;
  - use a suitable structure and style of writing.

The Contemporary Issues questions—only answer 3 questions. To answer more wastes time

Advice

- You are advised not to spend more than 25 minutes on each Question.

It is important to read all of this—it tells you what to do and what not to do

2

SECTION A
Truth and Spirituality

Answer **Question 1** in the spaces provided.

A 1 Truth and Spirituality   **Total for this question:** *20 marks*

Read the following statements and then answer the questions below.

Statement A:	I'm religious. My holy book and my conscience tell me what's true.

Statement B:	The only truth is what science can prove. Belonging to a religion is a waste of time.

Statement C:	There's more to life than science can prove. People are more than just machines. I'm not religious but I think we all have a spiritual side.

(a)   Look at Statement A.

Give one example of a *holy book*.

....

....

(1 mark)

(b)   Look at Statement A.

What is meant by *conscience*?

....

....

....

....

(2 marks)

3

(c)   Look at Statement B.

How does science prove something is true?

....

....

....

....

....

....

....

....

This means it could be a levels of response question, so remember depth and breadth

(4 marks)

(d)   Look at Statement B.

How would a religious believer argue against the idea that *belonging to a religion is a waste of time*?

....

....

....

....

....

....

....

Words in italics, are trigger words—the focus of, or key to, a question

(4 marks)

4

(e)   Look at Statement C.

Explain why it might be said that all people *have a spiritual side*.

....

....

....

....

....

....

....

The key word or trigger word. Don't explain what 'spiritual side' means, say why people have one

(4 marks)

(f)   "The only truth is what science can prove."

Do you agree? Give reasons for your answer, showing that you have thought about more than one point of view. Refer to religious teachings in your answer.

....

....

....

....

....

....

....

....

....

The evaluative question—you must answer from at least 2 points of view to get more than 3 marks

(5 marks)

5

These will all be 'structured essay' questions, which means all parts of the question are linked

Read all, then choose which 3 you prefer or are best at

SECTION B
Religious Responses to Contemporary Issues

Answer **all** parts of **any 3** questions from **Questions 2 to 7.**

B 2   Matters of Life   **Total for this question : *20 marks***

(a)   Explain what is meant by *in vitro fertilisation* and why it is used.

(5 marks)

(b)   Explain what is meant by cloning and the relevance of religious beliefs to this issue.

(10 marks)

(c)   " There is nothing wrong with using human embryos for medical research."

How far do you agree? Give reasons for your answer, showing that you have thought
about more than one point of view. Refer to religious teachings in your answer.

(5 marks)

B 2   Matters of Death   **Total for this question : *20 marks***

(a)   Explain the work of a hospice.

(5 marks)

(b)   How might religious teachings and beliefs influence a person's decision about
euthanasia?

(10 marks)

(c)   "People have the right to decide for themselves whether they should to live or die."

How far do you agree? Give reasons for your answer, showing that you have thought
about more than one point of view. Refer to religious teachings in your answer.

(5 marks)

B 4   Drug Abuse   **Total for this question : *20 marks***

(a)   Explain some of the reasons people give for taking drugs.

(5 marks)

(b)   Explain religious attitudes towards alcohol **and** illegal drugs.

(10 marks)

(c)   "The law should not get involved in personal matters like taking drugs."

How far do you agree? Give reasons for your answer, showing that you have thought
about more than one point of view. Refer to religious teachings in your answer.

(5 marks)

Don't do all the questions. They will be marked, and your best scores counted, but you will have wasted so much time it will cost you dearly

On the sample paper, part b is always worth 10 marks. This may change, but you have to be prepared. Check back to see how to answer it

Turn over ▶

6

B 5   Media & Technology   **Total for this question : *20 marks***

    (a)   Explain the concerns which religious people might have about tabloid newspapers.

(5 marks)

    (b)   Explain why religious parents might control the television viewing of their children.

    (c)   "The media ignore people's spiritual needs."

        How far do you agree? Give reasons for your answer, showing that you ha
        about more than one point of view. Refer to religious teachings in your ans

Evaluative questions are worth 20 marks in total over the whole paper. So start practising—that is almost a quarter of the total

B 6   Crime & Punishment   **Total for this question : *20 marks***

    (a)   Explain why religious people might sometimes consider it right to break the law.

(5 marks)

    (b)   Explain religious attitudes towards criminals.

(10 marks)

    (c)   "Execution is less degrading and inhuman than keeping someone locked up in prison
        for life."

        How far do you agree? Give reasons for your answer, showing that you have thought
        about more than one point of view. Refer to religious teachings in your answer.

(5 marks)

B 7   Rich & Poor in Society   **Total for this question : *20 marks***

    (a)   Explain the problems that might be faced by someone who suddenly becomes very
        rich.

(5 marks)

    (b)   Explain religious attitudes towards wealth and possessions.

(10 marks)

    (c)   "It is wrong for a few people to be very rich while many are poor."

        How far do you agree? Give reasons for your answer, showing that you have thought
        about more than one point of view. Refer to religious teachings in your answer.

(5 marks)

END OF QUESTIONS

Glossary

Active euthanasia – ending the life of someone who is terminally ill, for example, by an action such as lethal injection

AID (artificial insemination by donor) – conception through scientific methods, but using the sperm of a donor (not the husband)

AIH (artificial insemination by husband) – conception through artificial methods

Artefact – an object that has religious or spiritual importance/value

Belief – to have a principle that is accepted as true without positive proof

Blasphemy – to show contempt or disrespect to God. A serious offence in many religions

Blood transfusion – receiving blood as part of medical procedure

Capital punishment – execution as punishment for a crime

Categorisation of films – giving a 'type' to a film, which then determines the age of those allowed to watch it

Censorship – a policy or programme to control the media (in the case of this book), either personally or by the state

Certainty – something established as inevitable and without doubt

Cloning – to produce organisms or cells with the same genetic constitution

Community service – punishment that involves working set numbers of hours on a project in the community, e.g. cleaning fences after the crime of vandalism

Deterrence – the ability of a punishment to put others off the idea of doing something

Drug abuse – use of drugs for a purpose other than a medical requirement

Early release (from prison) – when prisoners are released before their original sentence is actually completed, usually for good behaviour

Embryology – the branch of science concerned with the study of embryos

Euthanasia (mercy killing) – the ending of someone's life who is terminally ill or has no quality of life, for compassionate reasons

Evangelism – the practice of spreading the Christian message

Evidence – data on which to base proof or to establish truth or falsehood

Extended family – a social unit that contains the nuclear family together with blood relatives

Faith – strong or unshakeable belief in something without proof or evidence

'Fat cat' salaries – excessive salaries paid to people who are already wealthy

Forgiveness – the act of being forgiving or merciful to others

Gambling – placing money to predict a specific outcome, in order to win more money, e.g. backing a horse in a race

Hard drugs – Category A/B drugs, e.g. heroin, cocaine

Homelessness – not having a place to live

Hospice – form of hospital that specialises in palliative care (care of the dying)

Human genetic engineering – experiments or modification of gene makeup to change features of a human, e.g. to remove an illness from the embryo

Icon – religious painting, painted by an artist who has focused on God during its making

Imprisonment – putting someone into prison as a punishment

Indolence – to not like work, show no effort, be lazy or idle

Inherited wealth – money and possessions that have been gained through someone leaving them to you in a will

Internet – the World Wide Web

Involuntary euthanasia – mercy killing, carried out without the patient's consent, because they are unable to give that consent, e.g. switching off a life support system

IVF – in vitro fertilisation, also known as 'test-tube babies' – an artificial form of conception

Life imprisonment – the most severe punishment for a crime in the UK, actually a set number of years not literally life

Life support system – medical equipment which can keep a person alive, by supporting breathing etc.

Minimum wage – a base limit set by the Government determining the minimum amount a person over 18 can be paid

Mysticism – branch within a religious tradition which uses meditation/contemplation to make contact with God. Often includes many secret rituals as part of this process

National Lottery – UK national gambling game, based on choosing the numbers that will be randomly selected

Nuclear family – mum, dad and their children

Parole – the freeing of a prisoner before their sentence has expired on the condition that they have shown good behaviour

Passive euthanasia – where someone is allowed to die, e.g. by denying them medication

Performance enhancing drugs – drugs that are taken to improve someone's ability in sport

Pornography – writings/films/pictures that are designed to stimulate sexual excitement

Poverty – the condition of being without money, food or other basic needs of life

Probability – an occurrence that is highly likely to happen

Proof – evidence that is given to establish the truth / validity of something

Protection – one of the purposes of punishment, to protect the criminal, society, or both

Punishment – a penalty or sanction that is given for any crime or offence

Quality of life – the state of living whereby length is not the only concern, but where the value and fullness of life are important

Recreational drugs – drugs taken in a person's spare time

Reformation – a reason for punishment given to change a criminal for the better

Religious tradition – a religion, or a denomination within Christianity. You should be aware of attitudes, or examples, from two different ones for any topic in the course.

Retribution – an act of punishment based upon revenge, the idea that the punishment should fit the crime

Ritual – a set pattern of actions/movements, which can be part of an act of worship

Sacred writing – holy book, e.g. Bible

Sanctity of life – the idea that life is special, even sacred, because it is God-given

Satellite broadcasting – channels accessible through a satellite dish, e.g. Sky

Sexual intercourse – the sexual act – the insertion of the male penis into the female's vagina

Social drugs – where an individual takes drugs as part of a social life with others

Soft drugs – Category C drugs

Spirituality – of, or concerned with, the spirit, not worldly or physical, connection with the church or religion

Suicide – the act of killing oneself

Surrogacy – when a woman becomes pregnant, and gives birth on behalf of someone else, who will then bring up the child as their own

Terrestrial television – the channels available through a 'normal' aerial – BBC, ITV, C4, C5

Transplant surgery – surgery to replace an organ with one from another person, because the original no longer works

Trust – to have a firm belief in the reliability of a person or thing

Truth – the state of being true

TV watershed – the time after which certain types of programmes may be shown because of their content, e.g. sex, violence, language

Unemployment – the state of not having paid employment

Vatican I and II – these were Councils attended by Bishops which discussed church teachings. Their discussions were codified into book form, named after the Councils.

Vindication – to clear someone of blame or suspicion

Voluntary euthanasia – euthanasia that is carried out because it is the wishes of the patient

Wealth – a great quantity of money or possessions

Website – a site on the Internet set up by a specific person/group

Whirling Dervishes – name given to the members of a Sufi sect of the Islamic faith, characterised by their dancing which leads to trance states

World Wide Web – 'www' e.g. a network of related or non-related sites of information via the Internet.

Wrongdoing – another word for 'sin'

Xenotransplant surgery – use of parts from genetically modified animals in transplant surgery

Index